BUSINESS AND ENTERPRISE

SECOND EDITION

Tess Bayley
Leanna Oliver

This resource has been endorsed by national awarding organisation, NCFE. This means that NCFE has reviewed them and agreed that they meet the necessary endorsement criteria.

Whilst NCFE has exercised reasonable care and skill in endorsing this resource, we make no representation, express or implied, with regard to the continued accuracy of the information contained in this resource. NCFE does not accept any legal responsibility or liability for any errors or omissions from the resource or the consequences thereof.

Although every effort has been made to ensure that website addresses are correct at time of going to press, Hodder Education cannot be held responsible for the content of any website mentioned in this book. It is sometimes possible to find a relocated web page by typing in the address of the home page for a website in the URL window of your browser.

Hachette UK's policy is to use papers that are natural, renewable and recyclable products and made from wood grown in well-managed forests and other controlled sources. The logging and manufacturing processes are expected to conform to the environmental regulations of the country of origin.

Orders: please contact Hachette UK Distribution, Hely Hutchinson Centre, Milton Road, Didcot, Oxfordshire, OX11 7HH. Telephone: +44 (0)1235 827827. Email education@hachette.co.uk Lines are open from 9 a.m. to 5 p.m., Monday to Friday. You can also order through our website: www.hoddereducation.co.uk

ISBN: 978 1 3983 6881 1

© Tess Bayley and Leanna Oliver 2022

First published in 2019.

This edition published in 2022 by
Hodder Education,
An Hachette UK Company
Carmelite House
50 Victoria Embankment
London EC4Y 0DZ

Impression number   10 9 8 7 6 5 4 3 2 1

Year   2026 2025 2024 2023 2022

All rights reserved. Apart from any use permitted under UK copyright law, no part of this publication may be reproduced or transmitted in any form or by any means, electronic or mechanical, including photocopying and recording, or held within any information storage and retrieval system, without permission in writing from the publisher or under licence from the Copyright Licensing Agency Limited. Further details of such licences (for reprographic reproduction) may be obtained from the Copyright Licensing Agency Limited, www.cla.co.uk

Cover photograph: © Prostock-studio - stock.adobe.com

Typeset in India by Integra Software Serv. Ltd.

Printed in Italy

A catalogue record for this title is available from the British Library.

CONTENTS

Introduction — IV
How to use this book — V

1 Entrepreneurship, business organisation and stakeholders — 1
- 1.1 Entrepreneurship — 1
- 1.2 Business and enterprise aims and objectives — 9
- 1.3 Structure — 16
- 1.4 Stakeholders — 24

2 Market research, market types and orientation and marketing mix — 29
- 2.1 The market — 29
- 2.2 Market research — 34
- 2.3 Marketing mix — 43

3 Human resource requirements for business and enterprise — 75
- 3.1 Human resources — 75
- 3.2 Staff development and monitoring — 84
- 3.3 Motivation — 88

4 Operations management — 96
- 4.1 Operations management — 96

5 Business growth — 105
- 5.1 Business and enterprise growth — 105

6 Sources of enterprise funding and business finance — 112
- 6.1 Business and enterprise funding — 112
- 6.2 Financial terms, documents and tools — 117

7 The impact of the external environment on business and enterprise — 143
- 7.1 The impact of the external environment — 143

8 Business and enterprise planning — 153
- 8.1 Business and enterprise planning — 153

Glossary — 164
Index — 168

INTRODUCTION

This book introduces the revised NCFE Level 1/2 Technical Award in Business and Enterprise for first teaching in September 2022.

Content areas

Throughout the course, you will study eight different content areas as part of the qualification. This book provides complete coverage of each content area in the specification:

- Content area 1: Entrepreneurship, business organisation and stakeholders
- Content area 2: Market research, market types and orientation and marketing mix
- Content area 3: Human resource requirements for business and enterprise
- Content area 4: Operations management
- Content area 5: Business growth
- Content area 6: Sources of enterprise funding and business finance
- Content area 7: The impact of the external environment on business and enterprise
- Content area 8: Business and enterprise planning

You must study all of these content areas.

How will I be assessed?

Non-exam assessment

Sixty per cent of your final mark for this qualification will be based on a non-exam assessment (NEA), which will assess your ability to effectively draw together knowledge, understanding and skills from across the whole vocational area. The non-exam assessment will target the following assessment objectives:

- AO1: Recall knowledge and show understanding.
- AO2: Apply knowledge and understanding.
- AO3: Analyse and evaluate knowledge and understanding.
- AO4: Demonstrate and apply relevant technical skills, techniques and processes.
- AO5: Analyse and evaluate the demonstration of relevant skills, techniques and processes.

At the end of each content area in this book, there is a sample NEA for you to practise these skills.

Examined assessment

Forty per cent of your final mark for this qualification will be based on an exam that will assess your knowledge and understanding of all the content areas. The exam will target the following assessment objectives:

- AO1: Recall knowledge and show understanding.
- AO2: Apply knowledge and understanding.
- AO3: Analyse and evaluate knowledge and understanding.

At the end of each content area in this book, there are some exam-style questions for you to practise your exam skills.

HOW TO USE THIS BOOK

The features shown below appear throughout the book to support your learning.

About this content area

A brief introduction to the content area, so you know exactly what is covered.

Key terms
Definitions of important terminology are included throughout.

Activities

Short tasks to help develop your understanding. These include individual, group and research tasks.

Case studies
Examples of how different concepts can be applied to businesses.

Remember

A bullet-list summary of the key points at the end of each content area, to ensure you remember the most important aspects and to help you with revision.

Test yourself
Questions to test your knowledge and understanding of the content.

Read about it

References to books, websites and other sources of useful information for further reading and research.

Practice questions
Practice questions to help you prepare for the exam.

Assignment practice
A summary activity that allows you to apply knowledge and skills covered in a content area in preparation for the non-examined assessment.

ACKNOWLEDGEMENTS

The Publishers would like to thank the following for permission to reproduce copyright material.

Picture credits

p.1 © Sabinezia/stock.adobe.com; **p.4** © Liliya Trott/stock.adobe.com; **p.8** *l* © Chris Willson/Alamy Stock Photo, *r* © ROBYN BECK/AFP via Getty Images; **p.14** © showcake/stock.adobe.com; **p.23** © TungCheung/stock.adobe.com; **p.28** © koss13/stock.adobe.com; **p.30** © Maxx-Studio/Shutterstock.com; **p.32** © Tidarat/stock.adobe.com; **p.33** © grafvision/stock.adobe.com; **p.36** © Chris Brunskill/Stringer/Getty Images; **p.56** © Lenscap Photography/stock.adobe.com; **p.57** © Michaelpuche/stock.adobe.com; **p.62** © IgorGolovniov/Shutterstock.com; **p.63** © Philip Hall/Alamy Stock Photo; **p.65** © Grzegorz Czapski/Shutterstock.com; **p.67** © Jonathan Weiss/Alamy Stock Photo; **p.74** © koss13/stock.adobe.com; **p.95** © koss13/stock.adobe.com; **p.104** © koss13/stock.adobe.com; **p.111** © koss13/stock.adobe.com; **p.121** © laufer/stock.adobe.com; **p.141** © koss13/stock.adobe.com; **p.149** © Rich Carey/stock.adobe.com; **p.152** © koss13/stock.adobe.com; **p.162** © Александр Беспалый/stock.adobe.com; **p.163** © koss13/stock.adobe.com

Text credits

p.4 Thirsty Café case study, www.thirstycafemarcham.co.uk/pages/meet-the-team. Reprinted with permission of Thirsty Café. **p.14** Baltic Apprenticeships, www.balticapprenticeships.com/blog/employers/cost-to-train-staff; **p.86** Learning and Development Case Study: Heinz – A training scheme full of beans by Mary Carmichael, HR Magazine, January 25, 2010. Reprinted with permission of Mark Allen Group.

Every effort has been made to trace all copyright holders, but if any have been inadvertently overlooked, the Publishers will be pleased to make the necessary arrangements at the first opportunity.

1 Entrepreneurship, business organisation and stakeholders

About this content area

This content area focuses on entrepreneurship, business organisation and stakeholders. You will learn about:

- Entrepreneurship — What it takes to be an entrepreneur, detailing the motivators and the skills and attributes that are needed in order for an entrepreneur to be successful.
- Business and enterprise aims and objectives — The various aims and objectives that will be set when starting a business, including both financial and non-financial aims and objectives.
- Structures — The different types of legal structure that can be formed when starting a business enterprise and the different characteristics of these structures.
- Stakeholders — The various individuals or groups that will have some interest in the business, the benefits of the interaction between these stakeholders and the impacts of any conflicts on the business.

1.1 Entrepreneurship

1.1.1 Being an entrepreneur

An **entrepreneur** is often described as a risk-taking individual, but there are many aspects to becoming an entrepreneur. Entrepreneurs have many skills, including:

- being able to spot a potential business opportunity and investigating it further to develop the opportunity
- evaluating the viability of a business opportunity. This means that when they have completed research, they can decide whether or not it is worth pursuing
- being able to understand the needs of the customers who may purchase the products and services of the new business opportunity. These potential customers are called the **target market**
- being able to organise all of the different resources that are needed to produce the product/service
- understanding the planning required related to the production process of product/service
- researching and obtaining the finance required to start and maintain a business
- making use of all the elements of the marketing mix — product, price, place and promotion (for further information on this, see Section 2.3)
- being able to manage the risks involved in starting a new business venture to make the idea a reality.

Entrepreneurs are individuals who are usually highly motivated to succeed.

Key terms

Entrepreneur A risk-taker who sets up a business or businesses with the aim of making large amounts of profit.

Target market A particular group of customers at which a product or service is aimed.

Figure 1.1 A successful entrepreneur needs the courage to be different

1.1.2 Entrepreneurial motivators

There are three key types of **motivators** that drive an entrepreneur:

- financial motivators
- personal motivators
- social and ethical motivators.

It is usually assumed that the key motivator for any entrepreneur is money. An entrepreneur may want to earn high profits, buy luxury cars and spend many weeks taking extravagant holidays. In recent years, however, a number of entrepreneurs have run a business not in order to make massive profits, but in order to meet their personal and social goals. See, for example, the case study on The Thirsty Café (page 4).

Entrepreneurs may decide to go into business for a number of reasons, for example to:

- have flexibility in their working life. Entrepreneurs often want to choose their own hours of work, set their own deadlines and have more control over their time
- satisfy their desire to be their own boss and set their own rules
- help others by producing products or services that will improve people's lives
- create jobs in the local area and help the economy
- learn new skills
- be able to give something back to other people, for example many successful entrepreneurs donate time or money to worthy causes.

> **Key term**
>
> **Motivator** Something that provides a reason for an entrepreneur to be successful.

Financial motivators

Many new businesses fail within the first few years, especially if they have not been researched properly, the product/service is not wanted or needed by customers, or the business has a lack of funds. For this reason, the first financial objective is to survive. If an organisation is not viable, it is likely to run out of cash very quickly. To ensure survival, an entrepreneur needs to ensure that:

- there is sufficient cash to pay business debts
- the business has access to sufficient sources of finance
- the organisation has a business model that is viable in the long term.

Once the business's initial survival has been secured, an entrepreneur will turn to making a profit. This is when an organisation's revenue exceeds its total costs. In return for the risk and hard work they have put into the business, the entrepreneur will desire high profits over a long period of time. The financial motivator for some entrepreneurs may be personal wealth. They may aim not just to earn an adequate income, but instead to gain a substantial personal wealth.

Personal motivators

For many entrepreneurs, profit is not the main motivator for setting up a business. They may be motivated by the desire for control over their

1 Entrepreneurship, business organisation and stakeholders

working life, the opportunity to work from home or the option to combine work with family life. Sometimes people re-evaluate their working life, which may lead them to want to set up a new business. Some individuals may feel that their skills are undervalued and they are not reaching their full potential. Others become bored with being told what they have to do every day and want to become their own boss. Another key motivator is the feeling of personal satisfaction from building a successful business. Owning your own business can provide great job satisfaction and independence and autonomy.

Social and ethical motivators

Some people may have a desire to escape from a boring or uninteresting job or have an intense desire to pursue one of their interests or hobbies. There are two elements to this: responsibility and helping the community.

Responsibility

There is a real focus in our world on sustainability and living in ways that do not harm the planet. This focus is also important for the business community, with businesses making purchasing choices to source sustainable materials for their products/services. Businesses are more aware of the environmental impact of their products/services, and customers are often open to purchasing sustainably sourced products even if they cost slightly more. This could relate to the processes involved in producing a product or the materials that are used to create it, for example recycled bottles and packaging.

Another aspect to managing a business responsibly is ensuring that it adheres to the government's National Living Wage. (For more on the minimum wage, see Section 7.1.1.) Many businesses choose to pay their employees more than the legal requirement as they value the knowledge, skills and experience that their staff bring to the business.

As well as paying employees, employers have a legal duty to provide good working conditions. This relates to the environment that employees have to work within. Working conditions focus on:

- how the business is organised, for example, whether it is a large or small business. This could affect how information is communicated and acted upon by the staff
- the types of work activities that an employee needs to complete
- the new training and skills opportunities available to staff, which will affect their ability to do their job and carry out new types of work
- the health, safety and well-being of the employees so that they can keep working to a high standard in a safe environment
- working times and holiday entitlement so employees are not overworked
- ensuring that employees have a good work–life balance with regular breaks and opportunities to relax outside of work.

Activity

Individually, write down your hobbies or interests. Then, in pairs, compare your hobbies or interests and answer the following questions:

- If you were to rate your skill level from 1 to 4 (with 1 being the best), what number would you give your skills at your hobbies or interests?
- How easy do you think it would be to turn one of your hobbies or interests into an enterprise activity?
- What equipment would you need to complete your enterprise?
- How much money do you think you would need to set up your enterprise?
- Who would your main local competitors be?
- Could you turn any of these hobbies or interests into an actual enterprise?

Activity

Research the current rates of the National Living Wage.

NCFE Level 1/2 Technical Award in Business and Enterprise

> **Test yourself**
>
> 1. Write a definition of an entrepreneur.
> 2. What are the three key motivators that drive an entrepreneur?

Helping the community

Entrepreneurs who want to make a difference or a change will often start their enterprises with a specific interest and make this their priority, rather than profit. Making money will still be a consideration as they will need money to keep the business running, but they will then re-invest this money back into the business. Examples of making a difference by helping the community could include working with a charity, helping older people, employing people who may find it difficult to get work or ensuring that everyone is treated equally.

Case study

Figure 1.2 Afternoon tea

The Thirsty Café in Marcham, Oxfordshire, opened in spring 2020 in the new village hall as a social enterprise business run entirely by volunteers. The core values of the business are to:

- provide an informal, welcoming and safe environment for the local community to meet
- serve good quality, affordable coffee, tea and refreshments
- facilitate and develop opportunities for community groups to meet
- offer a rewarding and constructive volunteer programme
- run an economically viable project with any profit re-invested back into the community.

It proved to be very popular, with the local community purchasing drinks and refreshments from the café, but then the Covid-19 pandemic struck and, like many businesses, the café had to close its doors. However, undeterred, the volunteers met and decided to offer afternoon tea deliveries to the local community, focusing on providing quality local produce. All customers received their ordered baskets of goodies straight to their front doors. These were popular and kept the business going as well as benefiting the community, as the volunteers could still offer their services and the residents of Marcham could enjoy a special afternoon tea in what was a difficult time for many.

The Thirsty Café is now a great success, opening several times a week to serve the local community as well as providing the catering for many village events throughout the year. The volunteers involved range from young adults wanting the experience of working in a café, to individuals who enjoy baking a range of cakes and biscuits on a regular basis, to kitchen team members who take it in turns to cook bacon/sausage baps on a Saturday morning and front-of-house volunteers who enjoy the interaction with the local customers. The long-term plan for the Thirsty Café is to open six days a week, to employ a full-time member of staff to run the café and, from the profits once they are made, to purchase items for local community groups such as sports and social clubs to benefit all the villagers of Marcham.

Source: www.thirstycafemarcham.co.uk/

Answer the following questions:

1. Explain what is meant by the term 'core values'.
2. Identify two of the main core values of the Thirsty Café.
3. What activities did the Thirsty Café introduce when the pandemic affected its business?
4. What are the long-term plans for the Thirsty Café?

1.1.3 Entrepreneurial skills and attributes

Entrepreneurs need a wide range of skills and attributes to enable them to set up their own enterprise activity. A person will learn **skills** through their work, training, life and education. **Attributes** are qualities that some people naturally have, such as being confident in the presence of others.

Skills

The skills that an entrepreneur will need are explained below.

Financial skills

It is important that the entrepreneur understands the importance of financial management to ensure that they have sufficient cash to pay business debts, they have access to funds when required and the enterprise has a business model that is viable for its long-term survival.

Communication skills

Entrepreneurs need to get their product or service ideas known, by talking face to face with investors or people who can promote the business, making telephone or video calls to people, or communicating via email or social media platforms. Possessing good communication skills will demonstrate to others that the entrepreneur is confident and competent, thereby establishing important trust with others who will hopefully invest in their business or become their customers.

Management skills

Management skills are important to ensure that the business can operate and continue to grow for many years into the future. As the business increases in size, more employees may need to be employed. The entrepreneur must be able to manage staff effectively, ensuring that they represent the company and work towards making the business a success. The entrepreneur must also be sure to invest in their staff by increasing their skills and developing them.

Sales skills

Being able to develop and grow an enterprise activity is important, and to achieve this an entrepreneur needs to persuade potential customers to purchase their products or services. If products do not appeal to customers then sales will not be made, which would be a disaster for the business! Having good sales skills is vital for the growth of the business.

IT skills

Many businesses now have an online presence, meaning that customers can view and purchase products/services online. An entrepreneur

> **Key terms**
>
> **Skills** The ability of an individual to do a task well.
>
> **Attributes** Qualities that a person naturally possesses which make them individual.

therefore needs to have the IT skills to develop this presence or to give others instructions to do this, so that they can compete with other similar businesses. IT is also used to track the business's finances, stock control and plans for the future, and for marketing and networking with other businesses.

Timekeeping skills

There are two aspects to timekeeping:

- Ensuring that if any orders are placed within a required time period, the business meets the deadline so that it builds a reputation for being accurate and trustworthy. Imagine if you ordered a birthday cake for a party, and the order arrived after the party. You would not use that business again!
- Ensuring that the business owner is not late for appointments with clients, as they could become the vital customers who help to build the success of the business.

Attributes

Attributes are qualities that individuals naturally possess as they are what makes them individual.

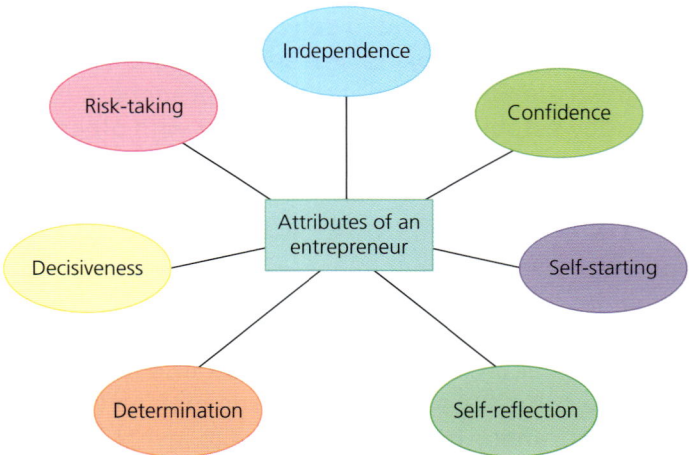

Figure 1.3 Attributes of an entrepreneur

Independence

Entreprenuers have the attribute of wanting to work independently from others as they are convinced that their ideas will appeal to the target market and want to 'go it alone'. By being in control of the production and selling of their products/services, they can make all the decisions and then hopefully enjoy the success.

Confidence

An entreprenuer will demonstrate confidence to everyone involved in their product/service, from the initial stages of development through to it being sold to customers. Demonstrating confidence means that an individual has expert knowledge of the product or service, focuses on its strengths, uses positive language when sharing knowledge with others, and has the ability to answer questions on the product/service.

Self-starting

Self-starting means that an entreprenuer has the ability to start something new for themselves, knowing that at times it may be challenging but being prepared to work through these challenges to establish their business. Entrepreneurs have the ability to celebrate every 'small win' related to their new business venture. This could range from seeing their first product being made through to the first ever sale of their product/service. An entreprenuer will often focus on the elements of success, however big or small, to keep them motivated. The end focus will be on the selling of the products/services to customers.

Self-reflection

Being self-reflective can be demonstrated in various ways, including questioning why a technique is or is not working well, asking for help from specific experts when required and scheduling time to review where the business is in terms of meeting its targets. An entrepreneur needs to be prepared to honestly evaluate where they are and where they need to get to in order for their business to be a success.

Determination

An entreprenuer needs to be determined and decisive, knowing exactly what has to be done and not hesitating to do it. This is because any delays could potentially mean that they miss out on an opprtunity that could change the direction of their enterprise.

Decision-making

Entreprenuers like to be in control, meaning that they can make all the decisions needed for their business entreprise. Any entrepreneur needs to be able to make important and often difficult decisions. They cannot be afraid to make decisions that may upset other people, for example if staff need to be made redundant in order for a business to succeed. As a business owner, the decisions will be made by them — these may be the right or wrong decisions, but the entreprenuer must take responsibility.

Risk-taking

Any new business has an element of risk, as there is no guarantee that it will be a success. An entrepreneur should be willing to risk investing both time and money into their new enterprise. They will have planned and researched their new enterprise activity but will also be aware that success is not guaranteed and it may ultimately fail. An entrepreneur will need self-belief to rely upon, maintaining positivity about the planned enterprise activity.

NCFE Level 1/2 Technical Award in Business and Enterprise

Activity

Some famous businesses have risked new products:

Google glasses were introduced in 2013 and again in 2017 as the next big innovation in technology, enabling the user to take phone calls and use the internet without the need for a smartphone. They were expensive, and exited the market very quickly!

Would you have bought Colgate Lasagna? The idea was that people could eat a ready-meal from Colgate and then brush their teeth afterwards with its toothpaste! Not many people wanted to purchase this item and it was withdrawn from the market.

- Research some other products from well-known businesses that have not been successful. Report your findings to the rest of the class.

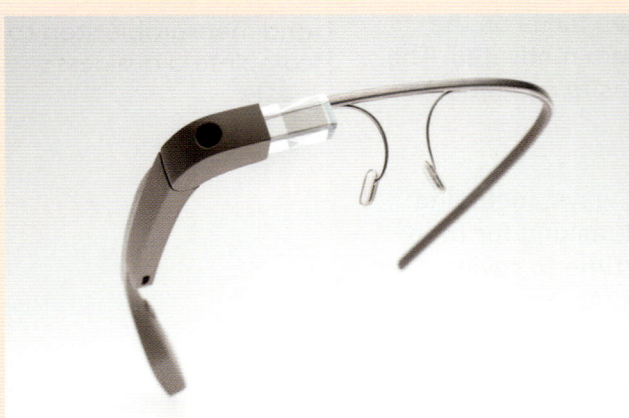

Activity

In groups of four, discuss the different entrepreneurial attributes and decide which of these your group members have. Feed back your findings to the rest of the class with explanations.

Test yourself

1. Identify two different attributes of successful entrepreneurs.
2. Explain how the phrase 'courage to be different' relates to an entrepreneur.

Remember

- Any new business carries risks.
- Entreprenuers must accept that their business idea may fail.
- Entreprenuers are often successful if they spot a gap in the market.
- A wide range of different skills are required to become a successful entrepreneur.

1 Entrepreneurship, business organisation and stakeholders

1.2 Business and enterprise aims and objectives

It is important for a business to set itself **aims** and **objectives**. Aims are the large goals that the business is striving to achieve, and objectives are the steps or targets that need to be completed to reach the aims.

Let's think about this qualification.

Key terms

Aim The goals that a business intends to achieve.

Objective A precise and measurable step to complete a business's goals.

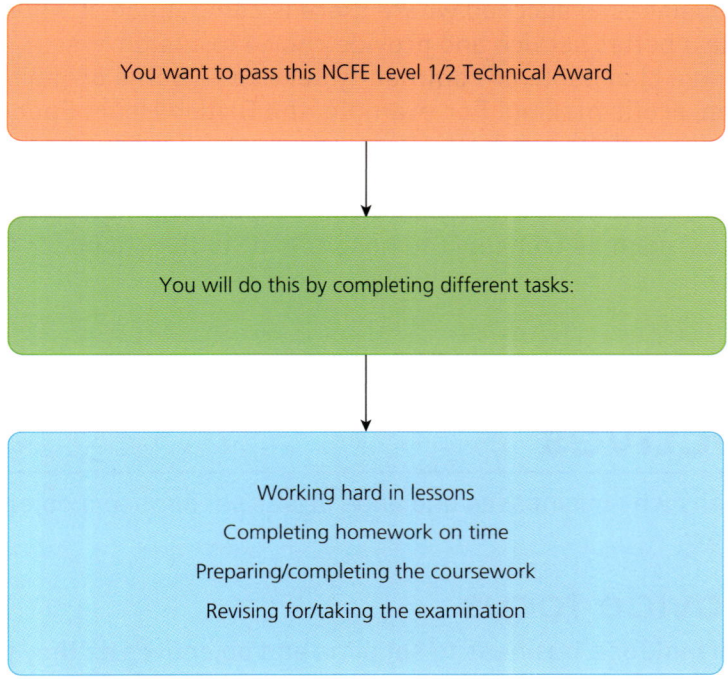

Figure 1.4 Aims and objectives

Therefore:

- the aim is to pass the NCFE Level 1/2 Technical Award
- the objectives are: working hard in lessons; completing homework on time; preparing/completing the coursework; and revising for and taking the examination.

Aims and objectives will differ from business to business, and the size of the business will influence its aims and objectives. For example, a small business that has just started to trade will often focus on gaining support by advertising its products/services, having excellent customer service and monitoring the sales of its products to ensure that it can make some profit. A large business that is established will have different aims and objectives. For example, to develop products that are more environmentally friendly, with the objectives being to change its current products by improving the factory methods used to reduce the amount of waste sent to landfill.

Other examples of business aims are:

- Survival — It is risky to set up a new business for the first time as often the individual setting it up lacks the knowledge and experience of running a business. It takes time to build up a customer base and generate sales, so surviving the first year could be a real aim.
- Providing a competitive service — Many businesses offer the same service and therefore a business may want to offer a better service than its closest rivals. Examples of this are supermarkets, coffee shops or barbers/hairdressers, which often open near their rivals. For a business to succeed where there is competition, it will need to provide a better service and provide choice to customers.
- Offering a charitable or community service — Some organisations are non-profit-making. For example, the British Heart Foundation has shops with its aim being to sell products that have been donated and to donate the money made to the charity for the benefit of others. Other community services include offering voluntary services, such as transport to hospitals or to the shops for the elderly.

1.2.1 Reasons for aims and objectives

The reasons why businesses and enterprises set aims and objectives are given below.

To provide focus

It is important for a business to set aims and objectives as they provide a focus for all the individuals working in the organisation for what they need to achieve in order for the business to be successful.

To inform a mission statement

A business will often set out its overall aims and objectives in a document called a **mission statement**. This is the business's vision for what it is striving to achieve. Producing a mission statement helps the business to plan for the future. The mission statement is published in the public domain and states what the business aims to achieve and how it will do this. It states the business's objectives, its overall values and the standards that it will set itself.

> **Key term**
>
> **Mission statement** A formal document that states the business's vision for what it is striving to achieve.

1 Entrepreneurship, business organisation and stakeholders

> **Test yourself**
>
> 1. What is the difference between an aim and an objective?
> 2. Decide which of the following is an aim and which is an objective.
>
> | | Aim | Objective |
> |---|---|---|
> | Improve a product | | |
> | Survival | | |
> | Offer a charitable or community service | | |
>
> 3. Why will a business create a mission statement?

Read about it

www.fond.co/blog/best-mission-statements — Information about the mission statements of a range of different businesses.

To help allocate resources

Setting aims and objectives means that a business can plan ahead with what it is trying to achieve. This provides focus for individuals but it will also ensure that the business can allocate resources. This involves a business planning:

- Land — Where the business will be based and how much space is needed for the business venture.
- Labour — The employees/staff needed, with the right skills, knowledge and availability to be able to produce the products/services.
- Finance — The finance needed in order to produce the products/services and how this will be obtained.

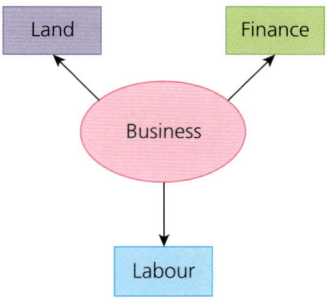

Figure 1.5 Allocating resources

To manage progress

Once the aims and objectives have been agreed, the mission statement has been written and resources allocated, the entrepreneur will need to ensure that the enterprise progresses to enable the aims and objectives to be met. They will do this by managing the day-to-day running of the enterprise and focusing on the aims and objectives to ensure that these can be achieved within the timescales that have been set. When aims and objectives are achieved, it is important to celebrate these successes. If they are missed, then the entrepreneur (and other employees in the business) can reflect on why this may have occurred and formulate plans to continue to improve.

1.2.2 Financial aims and objectives

There are a number of possible aims and objectives for a business related to finance. These could include:

- Increasing profit margins — Most businesses aim to make profit, with some having this as their main aim. These businesses are known as **profit maximisers**. Other businesses might want to make a satisfactory profit and to increase this each year. Making a profit allows for further investment in the business, which could mean expansion or rewarding employees with bonuses.
- Increasing **revenue** — Revenue is the money that a business makes from selling its goods and services. If the enterprise is successful, this can put the business in a much stronger position in its specific market, making it more dominant and further increasing its revenue.
- Increasing the value of the business — If the business is successful at selling its products/services, the revenue it generates and its profit margins will increase. This also means that the business will be worth more money. For example, if a person starts a small company and every year for five years it increases its revenue and profits, the business will increase in value and be worth more money to the business owner. They could then decide to sell the business to someone else and make a profit.
- Reducing costs — If a business reduces its costs, it will be able to increase its profits. It could do this by reducing the amount that it prints to save on paper costs or by adopting a more environmentally friendly approach to generating electricity, such as using wind or solar power.
- Improving liquidity — Liquidity is the way a business is able to turn the things that it owns, known as assets, into cash for the business. For example, a business that sells hats will sell these for cash. This cash is then used to manufacture or purchase more hats to sell and then to pay for other business expenses. It is vital that a business plans carefully to ensure that it has enough money, so improving its liquidity will help with this process.

Key terms

Profit maximisers When the main aim of a business is to make profit.
Revenue The money that a business makes from selling its products/services.

1 Entrepreneurship, business organisation and stakeholders

1.2.3 Non-financial aims and objectives

Non-financial aims and objectives are those that do not result in a specific financial gain for the business enterprise but will impact in other ways on its operations. These include:

Figure 1.6 Non-financial aims and objectives

- Positive reputation — A business that can provide a consistently good service to its customers or supply products that are good quality and value for money, and treat its employees and customers well will earn a positive reputation. This can be worth a lot to a business as individuals will recommend the business to their friends who may then purchase the products/services too.
- Increase market share — Market share is the percentage of sales within a particular market that a business has gained during a specific time period. Some businesses can dominate a market, which means they have the largest share of sales out of all competitors. If a business wants to increase its market share, it will have to implement changes. For example, a business might reduce the price of its product/service
- Sustainability — Sustainability refers to businesses completing their activities without negatively impacting the environment, community or society as a whole. Many businesses focus some of their aims and objectives on trying to ensure that their business is sustainable by:
  - reducing their **carbon footprint**, which means consuming less energy to help the environment
  - ethically sourcing materials, contractors or suppliers by considering where they come from. One way of doing this is to use local businesses to produce the required materials so that less fuel is needed to transport items to the business. This will reduce the impact on the environment
  - Reducing the amount of waste that the business produces either by reducing the amount of materials that are used to make its products or to provide its services or by recycling resources the business consumes, for example paper, packaging, etc.

> **Key term**
>
> **Carbon footprint** The amount of carbon dioxide released into the atmosphere as a result of the activities of a business.

NCFE Level 1/2 Technical Award in Business and Enterprise

Case study

A bunting-making business used to make four triangles from each piece of material.

Figure 1.7 Wasteful production of bunting

This created lots of wasted material so it reviewed its production process. It worked out that it could create more than twice as many triangles and reduce waste while still using the same size piece of material.

Figure 1.8 Reduced waste when producing bunting

By changing its production methods, it was able to produce more triangles for its bunting and reduce its waste, and, at the same time, save the business money.

Figure 1.9 Final product

Activity

The COP20 summit that took place in Glasgow in November 2021 brought together most of the world's nations, with the focus being to address and agree the key actions needed to address climate change.

- Research the findings of the summit and the agreements that were made as a result of the conference. Report your findings back to the rest of your class.

Read about it

www.gov.uk/guidance/equality-act-2010-guidance — Further information about the Equality Act 2010.

- Support for local businesses — Local businesses are vital to the economy as they provide services, jobs and security to their employees and put money back into the local economy through sales. Therefore it's important that local residents support them. If businesses use local suppliers, this also supports the local economy and reduces the business's carbon footprint.
- Support for equality and diversity in the workplace — Treating everyone the same is very important within a business. If employees do not feel that they are valued the success of the business could be compromised. By law, a business has to adhere to the Equality Act 2010, which legally protects people from any form of discrimination in the workplace and in wider society. This Act explains the many ways in which it is unlawful to treat someone and UK businesses need to abide by it and implement it in their operations.
- Reduce employee turnover — When new employees start in a business, it is important to invest in them so that they remain with the company. According to government figures in 2020, the average cost of training a new employee was £1530. So, if a business recruited ten new members of staff a year, it would cost it on average £15,300 to train them. If these ten people left within one year, the business would have to. If a business invests in its employees by making sure they are motivated, feel valued and are provided with promotional opportunities, its employee turnover, and the costs involved in this, would reduce. Having a dedicated workforce will provide stability and allow the business to grow with individuals who all believe in its aims and objectives (source: www.balticapprenticeships.com/blog/employers/cost-to-train-staff).

1 Entrepreneurship, business organisation and stakeholders

Test yourself

1. Identify two forms of non-financial aims and objectives.
2. Why is it important to support local businesses?

Activity

Look at the following graph from October 2021 of supermarket market share.
- Which supermarket had the biggest market share?
- Which supermarket had the lowest percentage of market share?
- What percentage market share did Lidl have?
- Do any of these statistics surprise you? Explain your answer.

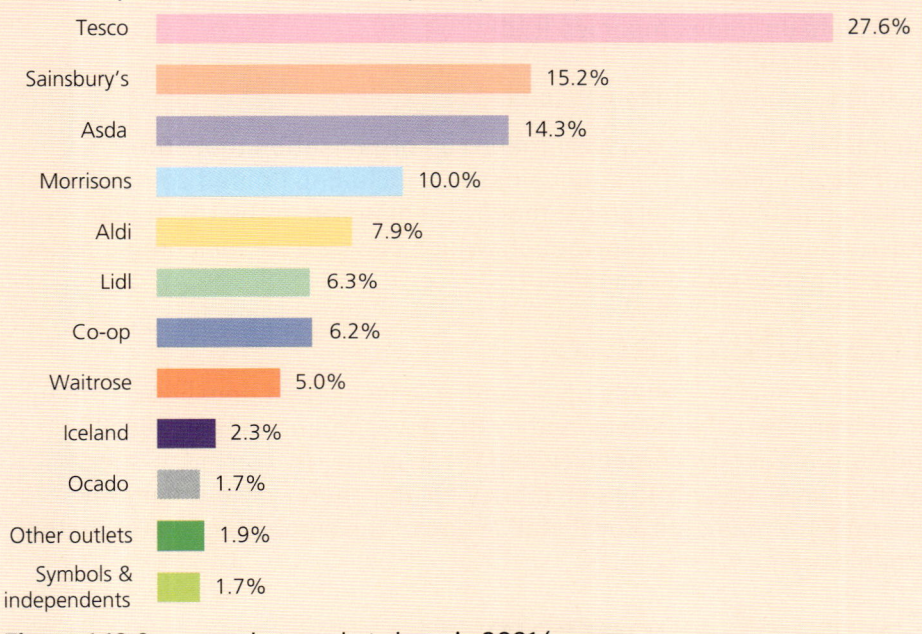

Figure 1.10 Supermarket market share in 2021 (source: www.kantarworldpanel.com/en/grocery-market-share/great-britain/snapshot/31.10.21)

Remember

- It is important for a business to set itself both aims and objectives as they give the opportunity for all involved to work towards these important goals.
- Financial aims and objectives provide a financial focus for the business.
- Non-financial aims and objectives are those that do not result in a specific financial gain but will impact in other ways on the business's operations.
- Businesses need to find their place in the market.
- Many businesses aim to be market leaders and to have a large market share.
- It is important that you are able to explain why businesses set aims and objectives and you may need to focus on a specific business that you are given. You may need to think about whether the business is succeeding or failing and why this may be.

NCFE Level 1/2 Technical Award in Business and Enterprise

1.3 Structure

1.3.1 Legal structures

The economy can be divided into two main sectors:

- the private sector
- the public sector.

The private sector

The private sector includes businesses that are owned by private individuals. Businesses in the private sector include:

- **sole traders**
- private limited companies (Ltd)
- **partnerships**
- public limited companies (plc).

Companies House is a government-run organisation that stores information on all different businesses, including limited companies and limited liability partnerships, that are registered in the UK. It inspects and maintains all the information, which can be accessed online by the general public and businesses.

The public sector

The public sector is made up of central government, local government, and businesses that are owned by the government. In the 1980s, the number of government-owned firms in the UK started to shrink as they were sold off to raise money for the country. Now, very few examples remain, but Royal Mail is one of the remaining public sector organisations.

Forms of ownership

The different forms of ownership for business start-ups, as well as their advantages and disadvantages, are outlined in the table below.

Table 1.1 The different forms of ownership for business start-ups

> **Key terms**
>
> **Sole trader** A business that is owned and controlled by one person.
>
> **Partnership** A business that is owned and controlled by two or more individuals.
>
> **Unlimited liability** When the business owners are personally liable for the debts of the business in the event that the business cannot pay them.
>
> **Limited liability** When the business owners are liable only up to the amount of money they have invested in the business.
>
> **Dividend** A share of the company's profits.
>
> **Franchise** A business where the franchisor (the owner of the business idea) grants a licence (the franchise) to another business (the franchisee) to operate its brand or business idea.

	Definition	Examples	Advantages	Disadvantages
Sole trader	A business that is owned and controlled by one individual.	Plumber or beauty therapist working on their own.	Easy to set up and low set-up costs. The owner makes all of the business decisions, which can reduce decision-making time. Sole traders can choose their own working hours and holidays. Limited legal requirements in relation to accounting.	Difficult for the business to grow very large due to the amount of money available to the individual and the amount of work one person can do on their own. The sole trader has no one to share responsibility or decisions with and may have to work long hours and struggle to take holiday. A sole trader has **unlimited liability**.

1 Entrepreneurship, business organisation and stakeholders

	Definition	Examples	Advantages	Disadvantages
Partnership	A business that is owned and controlled by multiple people. In most cases, there are 2–20 partners, but this number can be exceeded for professional partnerships, e.g. accountants and solicitors.	Estate agents Retail stores Building firms Catering companies	Greater capital investment is available from the different partners and risk and responsibility are also shared. Partners bring different skills and attributes to the business. Partners can discuss queries before finalising decisions. Bigger public image than sole traders.	Decision-making can be time-consuming as all partners need to be consulted. There is also potential for conflict. All partners are jointly responsible for the business's debt — like sole traders, a partnership has unlimited liability.
Limited company	A limited company is a business owned by shareholders and run on a day-to-day basis by directors. There are two types of limited company: private limited companies (Ltd) and public limited companies (plc).	Large public organisations, such as: ■ Manchester United ■ Asda ■ Barclays ■ BP	Greater capital investment available from the shareholders. Investors do not have to actively run the company. Bigger public image than sole traders or partnerships. Limited companies have **limited liability**.	Costly and complicated to set up. Limited companies need to be registered with Companies House. Annual accounts need to be published. Investors and shareholders expect income in the form of annual **dividends**. There is a possibility of takeovers if enough shareholders try to purchase shares.
Franchise	A **franchise** is a business where the franchisor grants a licence to another business so it can sell the brand or business idea. The franchisor owns the business idea and decides how the business will be operated and run.	Well-known franchise businesses include: ■ McDonald's ■ Pizza Hut ■ Starbucks	Limited business and industry experience are required, as the business model already exists. The franchisee owns the business but not the idea. As the franchise is well known, it is easier to raise finance. The franchisee benefits from the skills, advice and support of the franchisor. It is easier to gain customers, as the brand is already well known and recognised.	The initial and on-going costs of operating a franchise are not cheap. The franchisee needs to stick to the marketing activities agreed by the franchisor. May be difficult to break into a new area if competing with other franchisees.

NCFE Level 1/2 Technical Award in Business and Enterprise

Features of each form of business ownership

Table 1.2 Features of each form of business ownership

	Owners	Basic legal requirements to start the business	Liability	Responsibility for decision-making	Distribution of profit	Funding
Sole trader	One business owner	The sole trader registers with HMRC to pay taxation on profits made.	Unlimited	Single owner	Single owner	Sole trader's money Bank loan Overdraft Mortgage
Partnership (unlimited liability)	Two or more business owners	Each partner registers with HMRC to pay taxation on their share of the profits made. A partnership agreement may be produced to identify the key role and responsibilities of each partner. This may include how profits/loss are shared.	Unlimited	All partners equally unless there is a partnership agreement that states differently.	All partners equally unless there is a partnership agreement that states differently.	Partners' personal money Bank loan Overdraft Mortgage
Limited liability partnerships	Two or more business owners	Each partner registers with HMRC to pay taxation on their share of the profits made. A partnership agreement may be produced to identify the key role and responsibilities of each partner. This may include how profits/loss are shared.	Limited (see also section on limited liability partnerships on the next page)	All partners equally unless there is a partnership agreement that states differently.	All partners equally unless there is a partnership agreement that states differently.	Partners' personal money Bank loan Overdraft Mortgage

1 Entrepreneurship, business organisation and stakeholders

Franchise	The franchisor owns the business idea. The franchisee owns the right to use the business idea and the individual business that is set up.	The franchisee registers with HMRC to pay taxation on profits made. The franchisee needs to pay the agreed amount of money to the franchisor each year.	Varies depending on the franchise	The franchisor is responsible for overall decisions relating to the business design and idea. For example, store layout and brand logos, etc. The franchisee decides on working hours, holidays, etc.	The franchisee earns the profit from the franchise but needs to pay the annual fee and agreed profit percentage to the franchisor.	Franchisee's own money Bank loan Overdraft Mortgage
Private limited company	Shareholders (family and friends)	Documents need to be submitted to Companies House — **Memorandum and Articles of Association**.	Limited	Directors appointed by the shareholders to run the company on their behalf.	Via dividends	Shares from family and friends Debentures Loans
Public limited company	Shareholders (the general public)	Documents need to be submitted to Companies House — Memorandum and Articles of Association.	Limited	Directors appointed by the shareholders to run the company on their behalf.	Via dividends	Shares sold to the general public Debentures Loans

Limited liability partnerships

In a limited liability partnership, the partners in the organisation are not personally liable for the business's debts if they cannot be paid. Each partner is liable only to the amount of money that they invested into the business. This is known as limited liability.

Private limited companies and public limited companies

Private limited companies (Ltd) are owned by between 2 and 50 shareholders. One of the most important things about a limited company is that the liability of the shareholders is limited. This means that limited companies have limited liabilities; the investors can only lose the money that they have invested. None of their personal possessions is at risk.

Public limited companies (plc) are owned by a minimum of two shareholders; there is no maximum number. They have a separate legal identity — the company can sue and be sued, but it is the business that is sued and not the person/owner, as they are separate. Public limited companies are more complex to set up and have a minimum share capital of £50,000.

> **Key terms**
>
> **Memorandum of Association** A legal document that is signed by initial shareholders agreeing to form the business.
>
> **Articles of Association** The written rules of running the business, which are agreed by the shareholders and directors.

NCFE Level 1/2 Technical Award in Business and Enterprise

> **Activity**
>
> Barrie is planning to open a bakery business selling sandwiches, pies and cakes to local organisations. He is unsure of what type of business structure to choose.
> - Prepare a short report offering Barrie advice on his potential options.

Private limited companies can only sell their shares to family and friends, whereas public limited companies sell their shares on the open market to the general public.

> **Case study**
>
> M.H. Lee is a self-employed painter and decorator. She has been in business for the last 15 years and has established a number of loyal and repeat customers.
>
> To aid the efficiency of her business, she is considering forming a partnership with her friend Olson, who is a self-employed interior designer.
>
> Answer the following question:
> 1 Discuss the potential benefits and drawbacks of M.H. Lee and Olson forming a partnership.

> **Test yourself**
>
> 1 Write a definition of a franchise.
> 2 Explain the difference between a sole trader and a partnership.
> 3 Write a definition of the term 'unlimited liability'.
> 4 Identify three sources of capital for a private limited company.

1.3.2 The impact on business and enterprise of different structural characteristics

The organisational structure is the way in which a business is arranged to carry out its activities. This can be illustrated in an organisational chart like the one below.

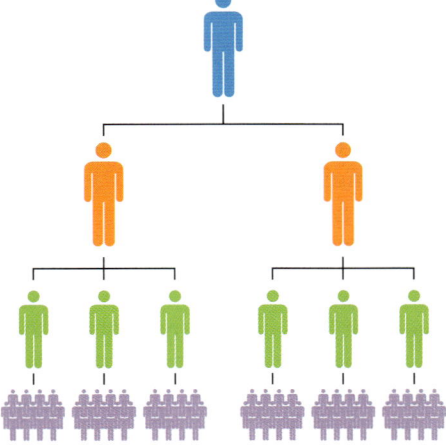

Figure 1.11 Organisational chart

1 Entrepreneurship, business organisation and stakeholders

Businesses frequently change their organisational structures in order to meet the demands of the current marketplace. Businesses need to compete with their competitors and organisational change is one way to reduce costs and expenses and to make the business operate more efficiently.

Levels of hierarchy

The hierarchy refers to the layers of authority within an organisation. Usually this is between the chief executive and the workers who help run the business by interacting with customers, who are known as the shop floor workers.

A business with many layers is known as a tall organisation, whereas one with few layers is known as flat.

- A flat organisation may look like Figure 1.12. Flat organisations have wide **spans of control** as one manager is in charge of a large number of people. Often this occurs in smaller companies where the manager can speak directly to their employees about tasks that need to be completed. An example could be a car garage.

- A tall organisation would be represented as in Figure 1.13. Tall organisational structures have narrow spans of control, meaning each manager is responsible for only a small number of other employees. This allows managers to keep close control over the work of the employees that they look after.

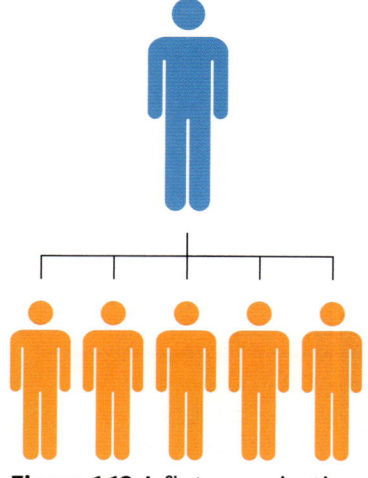

Figure 1.12 A flat organisation

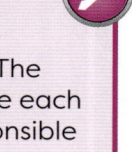

Key term

Span of control The number of people each manager is responsible for.

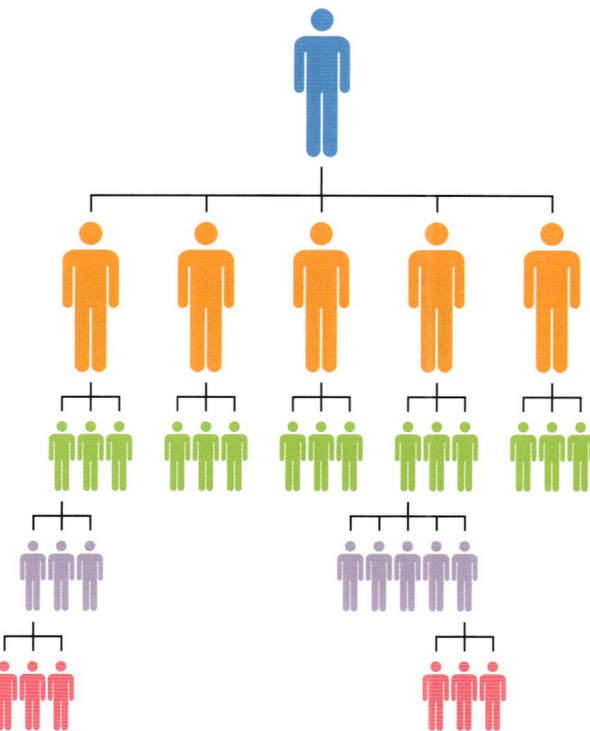

Figure 1.13 A tall organisation

> **Key terms**
>
> **Delegation** Allocating specific tasks to team members to complete by a given deadline.
>
> **Chain of command** The line of communication and authority within a business.

A manager may want to give some tasks to other members of their team. This is known as **delegation**. This means that individuals are officially given specific tasks to complete and report their findings back to the manager once completed.

As the control widens in a tall organisation, workers are likely to be able to operate with a higher degree of independence. This is because there will be managers, deputy managers, team leaders and other roles, which will have different responsibilities that require independent decision-making.

It is usual that a narrow span of control exists at the top of an organisation and a wider span of control exists at the bottom.

Traditionally, UK businesses have tended to be tall, with long **chains of command**. Due to the number of layers, communication is often difficult and decision-making can be very slow.

1.3.3 The impact on business and enterprise of changes in structure

At times, businesses may need to change their structure. Different changes in structure can impact on the business's operations in different ways.

Delayering

Businesses may remove layers (job roles from the organisational structure) as it allows faster and more effective communication. This is known as delayering. The idea was influenced by Japanese and American companies.

Reducing the number of layers in the organisational structure results in changes to the hierarchical order. This can improve communication within the business as there are fewer layers for the communication to pass through so it can flow better from the top to the bottom of the structure. It also can reduce the span of control that managers have, which can help improve control over their teams. Any changes in business structure will result in changes of responsibility for those involved, which can have a positive effect on their work within the business as managers may have more or less responsibility. A manager may welcome the increase in responsibility and the challenge of managing more individuals. Equally, a manager who has many staff to manage may welcome having fewer to manage as a result of delayering.

In recent years, many large businesses in the UK have taken out their middle layer of managers. This has been due to pressures for businesses to reduce costs because of the rising costs of products/services such as gas and electricity.

1 Entrepreneurship, business organisation and stakeholders

Redundancies

If an organisation reduces its number of workers, these workers need to be made redundant. The cost savings for the business of doing this are often very large because of the savings of wages, however the business will need to give these workers redundancy payments. The workers will then need to find other employment. The redundancy payments will help while they do this, but should only last for specified time period according to the legislation. Staff who remain in the business will often have an increased workload as the work completed by those who have left may still need to be completed.

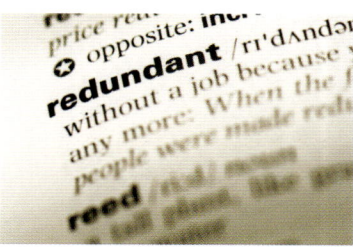

Figure 1.14 Reducing the numbers of workers requires redundancies

Reorganisation

During the life of a business, its structure may need to change. For example, a sole trader may decide to take on a partner to introduce additional capital and ideas to their business. Specific departments of responsibility may need to be introduced so that the partners have responsibility for different aspects of the business. Other workers may need to be employed as the business grows. This could result in further responsibility being taken from the partners and given to the new employees and new departments. This is a natural progression as a business grows in size.

Test yourself

1. Write a definition of the term 'chain of command'.
2. Identify two different forms of structure.
3. What is the difference between delayering and redundancy?

Remember

- The public sector is made up of central government, local government and businesses that are owned by government.
- The private sector includes businesses that are owned by private individuals.
- A sole trader is a business that is owned and controlled by one individual.
- A partnership is a business that is owned and controlled by two or more individuals.
- A limited company is a business that is owned by shareholders and run on a day-to-day basis by directors.
- A franchise is a business where the franchisor (the owner of the business idea) grants a licence (the franchise) to another business (the franchisee), so it can sell its brand or business idea.
- Private limited companies (Ltd) are owned by between 2 and 50 shareholders.
- Public limited companies (plc) are owned by a minimum of two shareholders; there is no maximum number of shareholders.
- A business with many layers is known as a tall organisation.
- When there are few layers in a business, this is called a flat structure.
- Delayering is when a business removes layers from its organisational structure to allow for faster and more effective communication.
- Reorganisation is when a business changes, for example due to an increase or reduction in size that affects the required staffing levels.
- Redundancy is when a business no longer requires staff, who will be given the legally required redundancy payments for their service to the business.

1.4 Stakeholders

A stakeholder is an individual who has an interest in a business. This includes anyone who will be impacted by the business's decisions. Stakeholders can include:

- individuals
- groups of people
- other organisations.

There are two main types of stakeholders:

- Internal — Stakeholders within an organisation, for example owners (shareholders), managers, employees and workers.
- External — Stakeholders outside of an organisation, for example customers, suppliers, shareholders, the local community, government and financial providers.

1.4.1 Internal stakeholders

Different internal stakeholders engage with a business in a range of different ways, as shown in Table 1.3.

Table 1.3 Engagement by internal stakeholders

Stakeholder	Engagement	Example aims and objectives
Owners (sole traders and partnerships)	The owners of a business are interested in how their business is doing, for example how much profit or loss is being made each year. Owners are then able to decide how much money they want to take from the business in the form of drawings.	To survive and make a profit by selling quality products and services to its customers.
Employees/ workers	Employees and workers need to be assured of the future outlook and job security of their employment. They are interested in the working conditions at the business.	Work hard, be recognised for the work that is completed and gain promotion when appropriate.

1 Entrepreneurship, business organisation and stakeholders

1.4.2 External stakeholders

External stakeholders are not directly involved in the running of the business, but support it in different ways.

Table 1.4 Engagement by external stakeholders

Stakeholder	Engagement	Example aims and objectives
Customers	Customers need to be certain that a business is going to sell them quality products at a price that they perceive to be 'value for money'.	Be able to purchase quality products/services with ease from businesses that appeal to the individual.
Shareholders	Shareholders in limited companies are interested in whether the business is likely to continue for the foreseeable future. They want to know that their share investment money is safe and how much they may receive back in dividends.	Support the business in a long-term way by investing personal wealth into the business. Shareholders will be able to vote at the **Annual General Meeting** that large business hold each year to inform investors of business plans for the future. Desire high annual dividends and would like the company share price to rise.
Local community	In many cases, the local community will provide the employees of the business. The local community will also be concerned about pollution, for example late-night noise or smoke pollution.	Provide quality products and services to the local community and add to the local economy by employing local skills.
Government	Businesses have to declare their financial records to determine their liability for taxation. In addition, government departments check compliance with various types of legislation, for example Health and Safety, Food Safety.	Support businesses when needed and encourage a more sustainable approach to business.
Finance providers	Finance providers, for example banks, need to be sure that any loans can be repaid on time and in full.	Support businesses when required and give up-to-date advice.

Test yourself

1. Write a definition of a stakeholder.
2. Identify some examples of stakeholders.
3. Explain the difference between internal and external stakeholders.

Key term

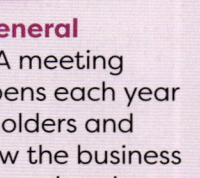

Annual General Meeting A meeting that happens each year for shareholders and details how the business has performed and the future plans for the business.

1.4.3 Stakeholder engagement

Each stakeholder group has its own particular interest in a business. By engaging with stakeholders, organisations aim to benefit from their skills and abilities. For example:

- Employees — Having a workforce that is fully involved in the life of the business ensures that staff are highly motivated and operate to their full potential. It is also likely that the staff will remain at the business and not leave for other jobs. This will increase the retention rate of employees. Fully engaged workers and managers are likely to have new and innovative ideas that can further the success of the business.
- Customers — Through engaging with customers, employees and consumer groups, an organisation has the opportunity to increase its sales and ultimately its profit levels.
- Suppliers — A business that fully engages with all of its stakeholders is likely to attract attention from new suppliers. This is because suppliers will be aware of their competitors and those competitors will want to work with other businesses, especially if they are well known. This could mean that the business gains a service and value for money from suppliers who compete for their business.
- Local community — By engaging with the local community, including local residents, charities, etc., a business increases its reputation in the local area. This could mean that the business attracts more potential customers, which in turn may lead to increased sales and profits that could be reinvested into the business. A business may want to join in with community events, such as Christmas fayres or summer festivals.
- Government — The government will celebrate the successes of businesses as it knows the importance of them to the local and national economy. A successful business provides employment, may attract tourists to the area (depending on the location), encourages investors, etc. This all adds to the national economy, helping the UK economy compete with the rest of the world.
- Finance providers — Finance providers, for example banks, need to ensure that any loans can be repaid on time and in full so that they do not make a loss. Finance providers can help with a business's planning and development. When a business applies for a loan, it is important that realistic repayment figures are devised as the business will not want to get into further debt. Engaging with the finance provider if repayments do get hard is an important aspect to this relationship that is for the benefit of all.

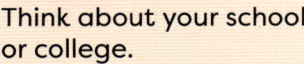

Activity

Think about your school or college.
- Make a list of all of the internal and external stakeholders for your school or college.
- In pairs, compare your lists and then prepare a table of how each of these stakeholders engages with the school or college.

1 Entrepreneurship, business organisation and stakeholders

1.4.4 Stakeholder conflict

Stakeholder conflict occurs when some of a business's stakeholders do not agree with the business's decisions or proposed or actual actions that have taken place. For example, local community groups will often oppose the building of new houses on fields due to its impact on the environment, but the government will argue that the UK needs more housing for the increasing population. This can lead to protests and can create bad feeling against the government and the housing development business.

Some stakeholders will feel that the aims and objectives of a business operating in a particular part of the country are incompatible with the local economy and environment. Examples of this include the controversial Heathrow runway expansion and the new HS2 high-speed railway.

Activity

Research the latest information on either the expansion of Heathrow or the HS2 railway. Produce a blog on your findings.

Remember

- Stakeholders are any individuals who have an interest in a business.
- Internal stakeholders are those within the organisation.
- External stakeholders are those outside of the organisation.
- Different stakeholders have different interests and engage with organisations in different ways.
- Businesses that engage with their stakeholders are likely to have increased staff motivation and retention, an improved reputation, new ideas and an increased share price.
- Stakeholder conflict can restrict business operations if ideas are opposed or blocked, for example the opening or expansion of business operations that could result in more traffic in the local area.

Test yourself

1. List two internal and two external stakeholders in your school or college.
2. Define the term 'stakeholder conflict'.

Practice questions

1. Select which **one** of the following is an advantage of being a franchise. [1 mark]
   a. There is less risk as products are well known.
   b. The franchise has unlimited liability.
   c. The franchise will use national advertising.
   d. The franchisee can make all the decisions.

2. Select which **one** of the following is the correct definition of a business objective. [1 mark]
   a. The large goals that a business sets itself and intends to achieve.
   b. A precise and measurable step towards completing the goals set by the business.
   c. A formal document that states the business's vision for what it is striving to achieve.
   d. The money that a business makes from selling its goods/services.

3. Select which **one** of the following is an external stakeholder. [1 mark]
   a. Worker
   b. Owner
   c. Employee
   d. Customer

Answer the following questions using the information below:

Ollie owns a fruit and vegetable market stall. He has been very successful over the past three years and has built up a large and loyal customer base, which has increased each year by 10 per cent. During the pandemic, he noticed that some regular customers were not buying from the stall. He decided he would deliver any leftover stock to these local customers. They were

27

always grateful for the fresh fruit and vegetables.

4 Ollie would describe himself as an entrepreneur. Define this term. [2 marks]
5 Ollie is currently a sole trader. State two features of being a sole trader. [2 marks]
6 Ollie would like to expand his business and is thinking about different options. He is considering changing his type of business ownership.
   a Identify **one** suitable type of business ownership. [1 mark]
   b Explain the advantages and disadvantages of this type of business ownership. [6 marks]
7 Expanding Ollie's business is a risk. Taking this risk may or may not work. Identify **three** characteristics that an entrepreneur must have when dealing with new business opportunities. [3 marks]
8 Identify three different stakeholders involved in Ollie's business. [3 marks]
9 What financial help could Ollie receive in expanding his business? [6 marks]

Assignment practice

At the end of each chapter in this book, there will be a sample NEA for you to practise your skills. They will be based on the following scenario:

You have had the idea of starting a sandwich and panini delivery service for companies based in business parks on the outskirts of your town. You are aware that since the pandemic, when many people worked from home, there have been fewer people working in the business park. You are writing a business plan for your idea.

Tasks:

Create a plan that details:

1 What structure of business you will set up and why you have chosen this form of business. (AO1, AO2)

2 The aims and objectives for the business. (AO1, AO2)
3 The various stakeholders that you will engage with given the type of business that you will be setting up. (AO1, AO2)

Read about it

Branson, R. *Screw It, Let's Do It* (Virgin, 2006) — Practical business examples and the lessons Richard Branson has learnt from running his businesses.

Jones, P. *Tycoon* (Hodder & Stoughton, 2008) — Entrepreneurial examples and how business dreams can be turned into reality.

Mawson, A. *The Social Entrepreneur, Making Communities Work* (Atlantic Books, 2008) — The importance of social issues in making organisations successful.

www.gov.uk — Practical information about how to be a successful business person.

www.socialenterprise.org.uk — A national body for social enterprise; provides excellent practical examples.

2 Market research, market types and orientation and marketing mix

About this content area

This content area focuses on the marketing that a business enterprise will need to implement if it is to be successful. You will learn about:

- The market — How a business enterprise understands its area of business, its customers and its competitors.
- Market research — The various methods that a business can use in order to research the market and how this information can be evaluated so that it can be used in the most effective way.
- Marketing mix — The 4 Ps of marketing, which are product, price, place and promotion. It is important that you understand each of the different elements, how they interact and how they are all important for a business that wants to gain a competitive advantage.

2.1 The market

2.1.1 Aspects of the market

It is important for any new or existing business enterprise to understand who its target customers are and which other businesses it is in competition with, through its knowledge of the competitive environment. Having this understanding will ensure that it can be successful within its sector of the business market.

Target customers

Identifying potential customers is important when considering a new business venture because a business will not survive without customers to purchase its products. Before starting a business, it is important that the entrepreneur spends time researching what other businesses are producing that may be similar to their business idea. They will need to offer something different that appeals to their **target customers** (who they want to attract), so that these customers buy their product rather than those of their competitors.

Key term

Target customer A group of customers with similar tastes at whom a business enterprise aims its products.

Ability to target particular groups

Specific products are targeted at particular groups of consumers, as businesses cannot produce products that meet the needs of every consumer. Targeting specific groups means that a business can concentrate on producing products that will appeal to them. Advertising will be targeted at these potential customers, who will react to the advertising and then hopefully buy the product.

29

NCFE Level 1/2 Technical Award in Business and Enterprise

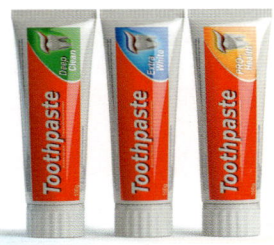

Figure 2.1 There is a range of toothpastes to choose from, all targeted at different customers

One way to illustrate this is to think about toothpaste. Most people use toothpaste, but there are lots of different types available, with different features that appeal to different people. When choosing toothpaste, a customer will have to decide:

- their preferred brand
- their preferred tube size
- the features that are important to them, for example best for teeth whitening, fresh breath or sensitivity, or suitable for children
- the price they are happy to pay.

So how do businesses target their products to customers? A number of different ways can be used, which are shown in Figure 2.2.

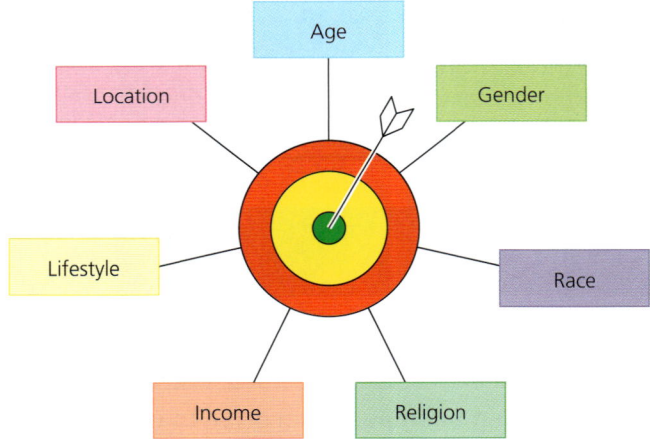

Figure 2.2 Different ways of targeting customers

Businesses will consider the most important elements of their products/services and then target the core customers who fit that target group.

Table 2.1 Different ways of targeting customers

Target	How it is used	Example of products
Age	Products may be aimed at babies, toddlers, young children, pre-teens, teenagers, young adults, middle-aged adults or those of retirement age.	Disney Store sells toys, games and clothing that are suitable for babies, toddlers and young children. B&Q aims its products, such as paint, tools and gardening equipment, at adults of all ages.
Gender	Some products are aimed at females and some at males; other products are aimed at both genders.	Make-up, fragrance and some types of vitamins are marketed to females. Haircare and skincare ranges are increasingly promoted to males. Radox makes a range of shower gels; they are targeted at different groups through scent, packaging and advertising.
Race	Some products are produced that will appeal to people who have a different culture or race, ensuring that they are culturally sensitive.	Some make-up, hair products and body decorations are marketed to specific cultures and races.

2 Market research, market types and orientation and marketing mix

Religion	A business may produce products for specific religious festivals and celebrations.	Products produced for Christmas, Eid al-Fitr and Eid al-Adha are examples of products for religious festivals that families celebrate all over the world.
Income	Products that attract a high price and that many people consider to be luxury items are targeted at customers with higher-than-average incomes; other businesses target customers on a budget.	Molten Brown produces toiletries that many consider to be a luxury product. Aldi and Lidl attract customers with a limited budget by offering cheaper alternatives.
Lifestyle	People spend money on items related to hobbies and interests they enjoy doing in their spare time, for example camping.	Go Outdoors specialises in products for people who enjoy outdoor activities, such as hiking boots, tents, sleeping bags.
Location	Customers can be grouped by where they live or work, i.e. their physical location. If this grouping was global, a business would need to consider time zones, climate, culture and language.	Products such as warm clothing and heating devices would be more popular in European countries compared with hotter climates, such as Australia, where consumers would be more interested in light-weight outfits and air conditioners.

Activity

Toothpaste is a product that we all use and there are many different types and brands available. In pairs, answer the following questions:

1. a Which toothpaste do you use?
   b Why do you use that particular toothpaste?
   c How long have you been using it?
   d Would you consider changing it? If yes, which one would you purchase and why? If not, why not?
   e What would persuade you to change your current toothpaste?
2. a Identify which part of the market you consider your toothpaste brand to be within. Why do you think this is?
   b Think of the type of toothpaste your partner chose and decide which segment of the market it falls into.

Feed back your answers to the class in a group discussion.

Competitive environment

Competition is good for business. Businesses review what other businesses are doing and change their current product and service offering to increase their sales and overall market share. If a business falls behind its competitors, it may not attract new customers and its existing customers may switch to a competitor. When completing a review of competing businesses, a business will focus on three different areas: price, quality and range of products offered.

Price   Quality   Range of products

Figure 2.3 Reviewing competitors

NCFE Level 1/2 Technical Award in Business and Enterprise

> **Activity**
>
> Research the brand Heinz: www.heinz.co.uk/products
> - What are the different ranges of products that it produces?
> - Estimate how many products it produces. How many have you tried?
> - If you could suggest one new product to Heinz, what would it be? Write a persuasive email to the company director describing your new product idea.

Price

A business will research the prices of competitor products to ensure that its own prices remain competitive. This means that its prices need to be the same as or similar to those of similar products. The business may also decide to investigate production methods that are more cost effective to the business, to enable it to charge lower prices (or make greater profits).

Quality

To compare its products with those of a competitor, a business will need to ensure that the products are of the same quality. Think about a simple coffee table. They come in all shapes and sizes as well as colours and can be made from a range of different materials. Prices vary considerably. However, is it really fair to compare a cheap coffee table that you must build yourself, with another that is much more expensive, comes with a 20-year guarantee and is delivered to the customer's home? The two tables are not really comparable, so this needs to be considered when reviewing competitor products and services.

Range of products

Many businesses produce a range of products, so they can sell different products to different customers. When businesses first start, they may just focus on one or two specific products to gain sales and profits that then can be used to expand the range of products offered. Competitor products could provide inspiration as to what products new businesses choose to offer.

Demand

It is important that a business is able to provide its customers with the products and services that they require, when they require them. This is known as customer demand. If customers all demand products/services at the same time, the supply of the product will run out, leading to a loss of revenue and profit. An example of this was seen during the Covid-19 pandemic, with the panic-buying of goods such as toilet paper, which led to shortages.

Figure 2.4 Panic buying of toilet rolls led to shortages

> **Key term**
>
> **Trend** A popular product which is in fashion at a specific time.

Certain products will be popular for a period of time. This is known as a **trend**. Trends are difficult to predict and businesses can invest heavily in what they expect will be the next trend, but which may not occur if customers do not want those particular products/services. However, it is important that businesses keep track of the trends within other competitive businesses and try to spot any gaps in the market that they can fill with their products so that they can gain some potential new sales.

2 Market research, market types and orientation and marketing mix

Case study

Figure 2.5 Loom bands were an unexpected trend

Loom bands were an unexpected worldwide trend that started in 2014. It involved people, mainly children, busily making and wearing chains of bands. Cheong Choon Ng was the founder of the Rainbow Loom business. He made a small loom board out of wood to help him and his daughters make rubber-band bracelets as his fingers were too big. He then went on to make a plastic version and invested £10,000 of his family's money to manufacture the product in China. It became a global success, with many celebrities being seen wearing loom bands on their wrists. The simple invention made Cheong Choon Ng a multi-millionaire.

Answer the following questions:
1. How were loom bands invented?
2. How much did Cheong Choon Ng initially invest in the loom band business?
3. What was the main difference between the original board and the one that was mass manufactured and sold globally?
4. Why do you think loom bands were such a success?
5. Research the loom band products that were made. Create a short article to explain the products that you find.

Test yourself

1. Write a definition of a target market.
2. Identify four different methods that a business could use to target customers.
3. Write an explanation of how each of these four methods of targeting customers is used by businesses.
4. What are the three different elements of the competitive environment?

Remember

- The target market is a group of customers with similar tastes at which a business enterprise will aim its products.
- There are three different elements to the competitive environment:
  - Price
  - Quality
  - Range of products
- Demand can be difficult for a business to predict.
- Certain products will be popular for a period of time. This is known as a trend.

2.2 Market research

> **Key terms**
>
> **Market research** The actions that a business will use to gather information about customers' needs and wants.
>
> **Market** Where buyers and sellers come together to trade goods and services.

Market research can be used for the following purposes:

- To understand the **market** — Comprehensive market research will allow a business to understand the needs of the market and then provide goods and services to meet those needs.
- To aid decision-making — The results of detailed market research can be analysed at management level within a business organisation. By analysing the results in detail, a business can make informed decisions based on the feedback received. The business could use research on customer needs, wants and aspirations to inform decision-making about the type of products or services it should provide.
- To reduce risk — Understanding customers' needs and wants will enable a business to reduce the risk by making well-informed decisions about products and services they should invest in.
- To gain customer views — Market research allows customers to discuss their views, needs and wants in terms of products and services offered. Once analysed, this information provides a business with a comprehensive overview of what needs to be produced and sold in order to meet the customers' expectations. Meeting these expectations will mean the business is likely to maximise its sales and profits.
- To inform product development — Comprehensive and accurate market research reduces the risks involved in launching a new product. Whenever a business launches a new product, there is the possibility that customers will not want to buy it. Market research helps the business to reduce this risk, as it will be aware of what its customers are looking to purchase in the future. Analysing market research information will ensure the products that are developed are up to date and meet the needs of customers.
- To understand how a good/service complements others in the market — It is important for a new business enterprise to research the products/services that already exist within the market, so that it is aware of how its new product/service will add to the existing competition. Understanding the market that the product/service is going to compete within means that the entrepreneur can make a decision about whether it is worth launching this new enterprise activity in terms of time and finance. Having this research information is therefore important and can help with future planning and give focus for the future.

2.2.1 Primary market research

Primary research (also known as field research) is when a business completes specific research itself. This research is often completed using questionnaires, observations, focus groups and/or interviews.

> **Key term**
>
> **Primary research** When a business completes original research that it needs for a specific purpose.

Questionnaires

Questionnaires involve a person responding to questions. This could be in the form of a written questionnaire sent through the post or via email, or online, or questions asked directly on the telephone, or using a personal survey completed face to face. It is important that these forms of gathering customer data comply with the General Data Protection Regulation (GDPR) (see Section 7.1.1 for more on GDPR).

Advantages:

- The information that is gained will be accurate and relevant.
- Questionnaires can be completed in a range of locations including at home, in the workplace, on the street or at the entrance to a store.
- Telephone, postal or online surveys could cover a wide geographical area.
- They are relatively cheap and quick to produce.

Disadvantages:

- Questionnaires can be seen as junk mail and therefore not be completed.
- Question clarification cannot be sought for postal or online surveys.
- Personal or telephone surveys are expensive to complete and time-consuming. This is because the business will either have to pay external people to carry out the research or use internal staff for the work, taking them away from their main job.
- Detailed answers are often lacking from questionnaires or surveys that are completed independently.

Observations

Observations involve watching and noting down what individuals do and how they behave in a particular situation. Retail stores frequently use this method of research, with the aim of providing the most effective and efficient store layout. There are two forms of observation:

- Disguised, which is when customers do not know the observations are happening.
- Non-disguised, which is when the observation is seen by the customers.

A business must assess whether the cost of completing the observation is worth the information it is likely to gain.

Advantages:

- If one aisle in a store had made few sales during the previous month, an observation may identify whether customers were avoiding the aisle entirely or just not purchasing those particular goods on those shelves.

Disadvantages:

- While an observation may identify what is happening, it will not provide the reasons why this is happening.
- Completing any observation is time-consuming and therefore costly.

Focus groups

A small group of individuals is chosen, based on the needs of the business conducting the market research. They are usually chosen to represent a cross-section of the public to ensure a wide range of views. The group then discusses key questions and themes that have been identified by the business. **Focus groups** can be completed in two different settings — face to face or online, with users for example accessing a video conferencing software. Focus groups can be very useful as they often produce high-quality, in-depth research information about the individuals' views.

> **Key term**
>
> **Focus group** A group of consumers who come together to talk about their experiences, thoughts and opinions.

Advantages:

- The information gained will be accurate and relevant.
- If needed, a co-ordinator can explain the questions or direct the conversation.

Disadvantages:

- Focus groups are expensive and extremely time-consuming to complete.

Case study

Figure 2.6 Burnley FC's match day mascot, Bertie Bee

Professional football clubs are keen to provide access for all. In recent years, they have introduced focus groups to discuss with fans what their needs and wants are. Following such focus groups, the football clubs have introduced a wide range of initiatives to increase supporter enjoyment. These have included: fan zones that are open prior to games, family areas, match day mascot opportunities, etc.

Answer the following question:

1. In small groups, identify a local professional sports team. Discuss potential initiatives that could be discussed should a focus group be held with its fans.

2 Market research, market types and orientation and marketing mix

Interviews

A business may decide to interview a range of different individuals to gain information to help the business. In preparation for the interviews the business will need to devise suitable questions to ask the interviewees. Sometimes a business may offer a small incentive to the interviewees for participating, such as a voucher or free products. Once the questions have been devised, the business will decide which form of interview it will complete, e.g. face-to-face, online or telephone interviews. This could depend on the resources that the business has available.

Advantages:

- The information that is gained will be specific to the needs of the business.
- The interviews can be completed in a range of locations, including in interviewees' homes or places of work, etc.
- The interviews can cover a wide geographical area if they are done online or by telephone.

Disadvantages:

- Interviews are expensive to facilitate and time-consuming.

Case study

Thomas Oliver wanted to start a homemade jam business. During the Covid-19 lockdown period he liked to pick strawberries at a local farm and found a passion for making jam. The costs were minimal for his enterprise. He was able to purchase wax disks and sugar in bulk online, to make his own labels and to source free sterilised jam jars by putting messages on a local social media page. Thomas tested the product on some friends who offered to complete questionnaires. Using the results, Thomas experimented with a range of different fruits, including raspberries, blackberries, blueberries and damsons. Having worked out his costs, he launched his Vibrant brand of jam in 2021.

Using the information in the above case study, answer the following questions:

1. Why did Thomas start his business?
2. What is the brand name of his business?
3. What research did he complete?
4. How could Thomas find out how to reach more customers to sell his jam?
5. Thomas wants to complete further primary research. Advise him on what method he should use and the reasons why.

Read about it

www.smartsurvey.co.uk/articles/primary-research-methods — Primary research information.

2.2.2 Secondary market research

Secondary research (also known as desk research) is when a business gathers data and information that has been collected before. It will often complete this research using the following resources.

Key terms

Secondary research Gathering data and information that has been collected before.
Census A survey conducted by the government every ten years to determine key information about the population.

Government reports

Government publications and statistics are readily available online to download. Depending on the information required, there might be a cost. The information is accurate and trustworthy, but it may be out of date. For example, the **census** enables the government to identify the social trends of the nation, such as understanding the type of people who live in different areas of the UK, but is completed only once every ten years. In addition, all government information will be generic and not specific to the requirements and situation of the business that downloads the information.

News articles

One of the most popular ways of collecting secondary data is via newspapers and trade magazines, which could be in either digital or physical format. These are relatively cheap to acquire, accurate and readily available. The information may be out of date, however, depending on publication date, and may not be totally relevant to the business.

Physical books, newspapers and trade magazines can either be purchased or borrowed from local libraries.

Competitors' data

Competitors' data may be available publicly, depending on the legal structure of the business. Any limited company has to publish its financial data on an annual basis. In the UK, this is submitted to Companies House and is publicly available. By reviewing the financial records of other organisations, managers can review their own business's performance. It must be remembered that for meaningful comparisons to be made, data should only be compared on a 'like-for-like' basis. This means that a limited company should not be compared with a sole trader.

Reports produced by market research agencies

A number of market research companies, such as Mintel, are willing to sell businesses research material. Before purchasing any research material, it is important that an organisation considers the quality of the material. It could consider:

- What will this purchased report tell me?
- Can I purchase just the part of the report that is relevant to me?
- Who is the author?
- When was the report written?
- Which report is best for me?

2 Market research, market types and orientation and marketing mix

Trade journals

Trade magazines may either be online or paper-based. The information from these sources is likely to be accurate and readily available. Trade magazine can either be purchased relatively cheaply or borrowed from libraries. However, the information may be out of date, depending on publication date, and the information collected may not be totally relevant to the business organisation.

Social media

Social media is another form of secondary research. Users post information about themselves, which can be a good form of research for businesses. The user can be targeted with specific advertising that is relevant to their physical location through their phone. Businesses can also use this method to advertise their goods/services and can track the number of views and 'likes'. These can be analysed and used as research. It is a quick and cheap form of research for a business to use but some users may find any further advertising a negative experience.

Online forums

These are places where discussions can take place with like-minded individuals. They are specific to different topics or themes that interest the users and can vary from recipe forums to sports forums. If a business was considering investing in a specific leisure interest, it may want to access a forum to monitor the comments that users are making, to ensure that its products are wanted/needed and will appeal to the target market. This would be time-consuming for a business to monitor but may provide beneficial information.

As with other secondary research, it must be remembered that the information could be out of date and not totally relevant to the particular topic the business is researching.

2.2.3 Data types

There are various forms of data that a business will need to collect to ensure that its activities continue to run successfully.

Businesses will need to have access to internal data, which is collected inside the business, and external data, which they gain from outside of the organisation. Both these forms of data can be qualitative and/or quantitative.

Qualitative data

Qualitative data is detailed information about people's opinions, views and thoughts. It is often gained by interviewing consumers. This data can be very useful as it can be used to ensure that the products or services sold meet the needs and wants of the business's customers. The way that this information is collected will depend on the resources the business has available, for example it may not have the time to ask customers

Read about it

www.bl.uk/business-and-ip-centre/articles/primary-marketresearch-vs-secondary-market-research — The differences between primary and secondary research.

Key term

Qualitative data Information that provides a business with an in-depth understanding of key issues, which can help when developing business ideas.

Activity

Individually, explain how a business that sells bread and cakes could collect qualitative information to help it with its business in the future. Write three questions to gather the opinions of customers of the bread and cake business.

direct questions. Examples of sources of qualitative data include newspaper articles, trade journals or social media. There are, however, other ways that the business could collect qualitative data, such as:

- observing customers when they are buying products or receiving a service, to see their reactions and review the process (observation)
- asking a group of customers to come together to talk about their experiences, thoughts and opinions related to the enterprise activity (focus group).

Advantages:

- Opinions can be grouped together so that the business can understand the attitudes of consumers in this market. If the data is gathered from the business's customers, it can be used to make it easier to maintain good customer relationships.
- A business will often use a smaller sample size as the questioning will be more targeted. This will be a cost-saving measure for the business.
- Gathering qualitative data is more flexible because the format is less formal. Prepared questions can lead on to other questions to gain in-depth opinions, views and thoughts.

Disadvantages:

- The individuals gathering the data must be experienced, as follow-up questions will need to be asked depending on the responses given by the consumers.
- Qualitative data does not gather statistical information, so cannot be interpreted in the same way.
- Further questioning may be required, which would be time-consuming for the business.

Quantitative data

Quantitative data is factual information that is collected, for example about customers' ages.

While qualitative information provides a business with a more in-depth understanding of key issues, quantitative data provides data for statistical analysis and review. Examples of quantitative data include government statistics, the results of questionnaires with closed questions (questions that have 'yes or no' answers) and data from published market research reports.

Advantages:

- Quantitative information provides numerical data and gives an overview.
- The data can be checked, making it more reliable.
- Data analysis is considered to be valuable and often 'impressive' to the reader when reading the results.

Disadvantages:

- Quantitative data does not provide any information about the reasoning behind the data that has been collected.
- The data can be misleading if it is not presented clearly.

Read about it

www.nibusinessinfo.co.uk/content/difference-between-quantitativeand-qualitative-research — Quantitative and qualitative data differences.

Key term

Quantitative data Information that is useful for statistical analysis and review to aid business decisions.

Activity

Using the internet, research some quantitative information about your local area that would be useful for a small enterprise activity.

- Display the information in a graph. You can either draw it by hand or use a computer.
- Write a paragraph to explain what the information shows.
- Explain how the data could be used by the enterprise activity.

2 Market research, market types and orientation and marketing mix

2.2.4 Market types

Mass markets

Mass marketing takes place when a business aims a product at a wide-ranging market (a **mass market**). To operate in such a market, a business must be able to produce goods on a large scale. This requires high investment in equipment and recruitment of staff.

Mass markets generally have:

- a high number of sales
- a large number of competitors
- products aimed at a large percentage of the market
- non-specialised products
- low profit margins.

The advantage of targeting a mass market is that a business should be able to produce goods more cheaply and also benefit from economies of scale.

Key terms

Mass market A large, wide ranging market, usually with high sales and many competitors.

Niche market A small, specialist market, usually with low sales and fewer competitors.

Niche markets

Targeting a niche market involves a business aiming a product at a particular, often tiny, segment of a market.

Niche markets generally have:

- low sales volume
- a small number of competitors
- products aimed at a small section of the market
- specialised products
- high profit margins.

The advantages of operating in a niche market include:

- A small business may be able to survive because it is offering a product or service that a larger organisation would find uneconomical to supply.
- Existing competitors might react aggressively if a smaller business tried to compete in the mass market. In a niche market there is less competition and any competitors are likely to be small.
- The business may be able to operate on a small scale. Many niche markets are relatively small and specialised. Small businesses are able to meet demand in the market, whereas they may lack the resources to meet demand in the mass market.

Activity

In pairs, think of a hobby or skill that is quite specialised and that could be turned into a business. It could be a skill that is in decline. It could also be something that you, a family member or friend are interested in and have the skill. Discuss this with your partner and share your ideas with the class.

Key terms

Market-orientated business A business that produces goods based on customer wants and needs.

Product-orientated business A business that produces only goods that it is good at making.

41

NCFE Level 1/2 Technical Award in Business and Enterprise

2.2.5 Business orientation types

Businesses develop their new products based on one of two orientations: market orientated or product orientated.

- A **market-orientated business** produces goods based on customer wants and needs. This is known as a customer-led approach. This business will undertake high levels of market research (known as being market research-led) to find out what customers want and need and will fulfil these with products/services. These businesses tend to be most successful, such as food and drink manufacturers.
- A **product-orientated business** produces only goods that it is good at making. This is known as a product-led approach. Such a business has low levels of engagement with its potential customers and so, although its goods may be high quality, they may not meet customer needs and therefore may not be easy to sell.

Activity

Look around the room. Focus on one item that you think needs to be changed and the reasons why. It could be that you want the chair you are sitting on to be more comfortable. If this is the case, how could you achieve this? Discuss your ideas with a partner and share the best one with the class.

Remember

- Market research is a vital part of any business success. It involves finding out information about the market in which the organisation operates.
- Primary research (field research) is the gathering of data and information that has not been collected before. Methods of primary research include questionnaires, observations, focus groups and interviews.
- Secondary research (desk research) involves the gathering of data and information that has already been collected. Sources of secondary research data include government reports, news articles, competitors' data, market research reports, trade journals, social media and online forums.
- Qualitative and quantitative data aid the research process.
- Mass marketing involves products being aimed at whole markets rather than particular parts of them.
- Niche marketing involves a business aiming a product at a particular — often tiny — segment of a market.
- A market-orientated business produces goods based on customer wants and needs.
- A product-orientated business produces only goods that it is good at making.

Test yourself

1. Why may a business be interested in the lifestyles of customers?
2. What are the two different forms of market research?
3. What are the two different forms of observation?
4. Which form of data are
   a) government statistics
   b) interviews?
5. How often does the census take place?
6. A group of individuals is asked to gather to discuss their opinions on a new type of bank account. What method of primary research is this?
7. Identify three different features of a mass market.
8. What are the main differences between market and product orientations?

2.3 Marketing mix

The **marketing mix** is the different factors that a business controls to influence customers to purchase its products. When a business markets its materials, it is important to consider the marketing mix (also known as the 4 Ps):

- **Product** — How the product/service is designed or invented to make it something that customers will want to buy.
- **Price** — How the product/service is priced to make a profit.
- **Place** — How the product/service is distributed to customers.
- **Promotion** — How customers are informed about the product/service and persuaded to buy it.

> **Key terms**
>
> **Marketing mix** The 4 Ps of marketing, i.e. product, price, place and promotion.
>
> **Brand** How a business is identified by others, such as consumers and competitors.

When marketing a product/service, a business will aim to integrate all four aspects of the marketing mix to create a suitable **brand** image. One individual element is not more important than the others, as they all link together. For example, a poor product is unlikely to sell, even if it is priced at a very low price. A business needs to ensure that its products are appropriately priced, promoted and placed in the market.

As the parts of the marketing mix are all linked together and have equal importance, to be successful a business must differentiate its product/service from those of its rivals, so that it stands out from other products. Another aspect of how the marketing mix works together is to satisfy those customers who the business considers will purchase its products/services — its target market.

Businesses need to make sure that the advertisements they produce for their product/service appeal to their target market. If the business selects the wrong type of advertisement, it could miss out on sales. Equally, if the product is priced too high or too low, this may have a negative effect on sales. For example, some customers may think that a cheap product is lower quality than an expensive one, even though this may not be the case. Conversely, if a product is too expensive, customers may not be able to afford it. If customers are unable to purchase the product/service because it is not available in their location, they might try a rival brand that is available and then be loyal to that instead.

The marketing mix, therefore, is crucial to the success of a new product/service for any entrepreneur and understanding the importance of each of the four elements is paramount.

Figure 2.7 The 4 Ps

NCFE Level 1/2 Technical Award in Business and Enterprise

2.3.1 Price

Price is an important part of the marketing mix. Market research enables businesses to make informed decisions about how to price a product.

Supply, demand and equilibrium price

The price of goods and services in a free market economy is determined by the interaction of demand and supply.

Demand

Demand is the amount of a product/service that consumers want. Changes in price will affect demand, as shown in Table 2.1.

Table 2.1 The effect on demand of changes in price

Price (£)	Demand
3	10
2	20
1	30

There are several other factors that also affect the demand for a product:

- Income — If the incomes of the buyers of a product increase, it is likely that demand for the product will also increase.
- The price of substitute goods — If the price of the product/service increases but those of substitutes stays the same, demand for the product/service will decrease and demand for substitute goods will increase.
- Complementary products - ones that are required in order for another product to fully function. For example, an increase in the price of cars will cause a decrease in the demand for petrol.
- Changes in tastes and fashions — For example, the decrease in demand for red meat in recent years due to the health risks it can pose and the increase in demand for vegan alternatives.
- Changes in the population — The population continues to change each year which can affect the product or services that we demand. For example, the ageing population will increase the demand for winter sun holidays as retired individuals can holiday when they want as they are not restricted by work.
- Advertising — A successful advertising campaign will increase the demand for a product.
- Legislation — Changes to the law will affect the demand for certain products. For example, the use of hand-held mobile phones while driving is illegal. This made hands-free mobile phone kits popular for a while, before the need for these was replaced by Bluetooth technology that is standard in most modern cars.

Key terms

Demand The amount of a product/service that consumers want.
Supply Knowing the amount of a good or service that is available to businesses or customers and providing this service.

Activity

Electric cars are becoming more popular which has increased demand for the products. Carry out research into why consumers are wanting these vehicles, making sure to use a variety of different sources. From the research completed, consider issues that you think someone wanting to purchase an electric car should consider. Make sure that you write down your sources of information.

- Research this petrol crisis further and share your findings with your class. You may have experienced this so you could also reflect on this.

2 Market research, market types and orientation and marketing mix

Supply

Supply is the amount of a product that suppliers are willing to offer to the market at a given time. A change in costs will affect supply. If costs of producing the product increase, the supply and quantity of the product could be reduced, as shown in Table 2.2.

Other factors that might cause a change in the level of supply include:

- The cost of production — For example, if new technology is more efficient, this will use less electricity and reduce production costs.
- The weather — Affects the amount of agricultural produce available for sale.
- Taxation — If firms are taxed highly on a certain product, they will offer less for sale.

Table 2.2 The effect on quantity supplied of changes in costs

Costs (£)	Quantity supplied
3	10
2	20
1	30

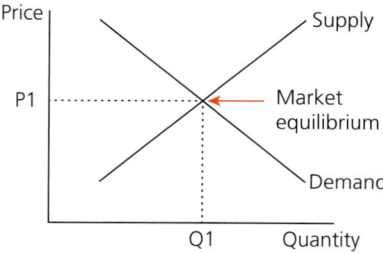

Figure 2.8 Equilibrium price

> **Key term**
>
> **Equilibrium price** The price that a business should charge for its product.

Equilibrium price

The price at which the demand and supply curves intersect is known as the **equilibrium price**, when price means supply and demand will be equal. This is the price that a business should charge for its product.

Dynamic pricing

Dynamic pricing is when a business varies the price for a product/service to reflect changing market conditions, such as charging a higher price when the product is more in demand compared to a lower price when it is not as popular.

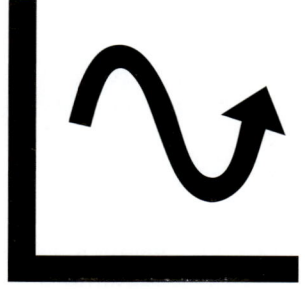

Figure 2.9 Dynamic pricing

Cost-plus pricing

In general terms, a business prices its product by working out what it costs to buy or make the product/service and then adding the amount of profit it would like to make. There is little point in selling a product for a lower price than it has cost to produce as the business would make a loss.

Figure 2.10 Calculation of selling price

45

Types of pricing strategies and the appropriateness of each

A business also has other considerations when pricing their products/services. It can adopt various pricing strategies when selling to customers, as shown in Table 2.3.

Table 2.3 Pricing strategies

Pricing strategy	Target market	Tactic	Advantages	Disadvantages
Price skimming	New customers	The business introduces the product at a high price and then gradually lowers it over time. For example, when Dyson introduced its bagless cleaner there was no competitor, so it could charge very high prices.	High prices can give a product a good image. A good image can lead customers to think the product is of very high quality. Gives businesses high profits while the price is high. This additional money helps pay back research costs that have been incurred.	Sales can be lost if customers are put off by the higher price, which reduces revenue. There is a possibility that competitors will bring out lower-priced products and therefore sales will be lost.
Penetration pricing	New customers	The business introduces the product at a lower price than competitors to attract customers. It then gradually increases the price over time. For example, selling a new flavour of crisps at half the price they will be sold at eventually.	Attracts customers to a particular product and attempts to make them purchase it. Is effective in quickly increasing market share.	Revenue is lost while selling at the lower cost, therefore profit margins are lower. Products that have a very short lifespan, for example fashion clothing, are not suited to this method of pricing as by the time the price rises, the product is no longer in fashion.
Loss leader pricing	New and existing customers	The business is willing to make a loss on a product in order to get customers to purchase it. The business then increases the price once the customers like the product.	Attracts customers as it is perceived as a good deal. This may increase customer numbers, revenue and profit margins. Products are sold for only a very small amount less than was originally planned.	Difficult to ensure customers will continue to purchase the products once the selling price increases.

2 Market research, market types and orientation and marketing mix

Competitive pricing	New and existing customers	The business sets a price that is similar to that of its competitors. For example, supermarkets price matching goods.	May attract new customers as the price is the same as their usual retailer.	There is no price competition as all businesses are charging the same price, which could damage the business's ability to compete. Profit margins are likely to be low as the selling price may only be sufficient to cover the production costs of the goods. Businesses need to be creative in their methods of attracting customers, as the price alone will not encourage customers to the store.
Promotional pricing	New and existing customers	The business temporarily reduces the price of a product to increase interest in it.	Attracts customers to a particular product and attempts to make them purchase it. Effective in quickly increasing market share.	Revenue is lost while selling at the lower cost, therefore profit margins are lower. Products that have a very short lifespan, for example fashion clothing, are not suited to this method of pricing as by the time the price rises, the product is no longer in fashion.

Key terms

Price skimming
Introducing a product at a high price, then gradually lowering the price over time.

Penetration pricing
Introducing a product at a lower price than competitors to attract customers, then gradually increasing the price over time.

Competitive pricing
Setting a price that is similar to that of the competition.

Activity

Fresh Food is a small supermarket based on the west coast of England. It is introducing a new range of salads.

- Analyse the advantages and disadvantages of the different pricing strategies that Fresh Food could use when introducing its new range of salads.
- Recommend which pricing strategy Fresh Food should use when launching the new range of salads.

2.3.2 Place

Place is the location where a business's products/services are made available to its customers. When making decisions about where to sell, a business needs to assess the cost effectiveness of each of the different ways that products/services can reach its customers.

Channels of distribution

Potential channels of distribution include:

- **Wholesalers** — Some producers sell their goods using a wholesaler. The advantage of using this method is that wholesalers buy in bulk and then resell smaller quantities of goods to retailers. The disadvantage is that unless the wholesaler is owned by the producer, profit levels will be lower as the producer will need to pay the wholesaler to sell its goods.
- **Retailers** — A retailer will place goods and products into shops so that customers can buy them. The advantage is that the products can be seen and touched by the potential customers who visit the shop. The disadvantage is that unless the shop is owned by the producer, profit levels will be lower as the producer will need to pay the retailer to sell its goods.
- **Direct selling** — Examples include mail order or website selling (also known as e-commerce). The producer sells its own products/services directly to customers without the need for a physical store. Producers often place their products in catalogues or on the business's website. The advantages are that products can be targeted and personalised to the customers. The disadvantages are that individuals could find the direct selling intrusive, which can lead to low response rates from the targeted audience and may also affect costs to the business.

Key term

Wholesaler A business that sells goods in large quantities to retailers at low prices.

Factors affecting place

There are several different factors that will affect place as part of the marketing mix. (See Figure 2.11.)

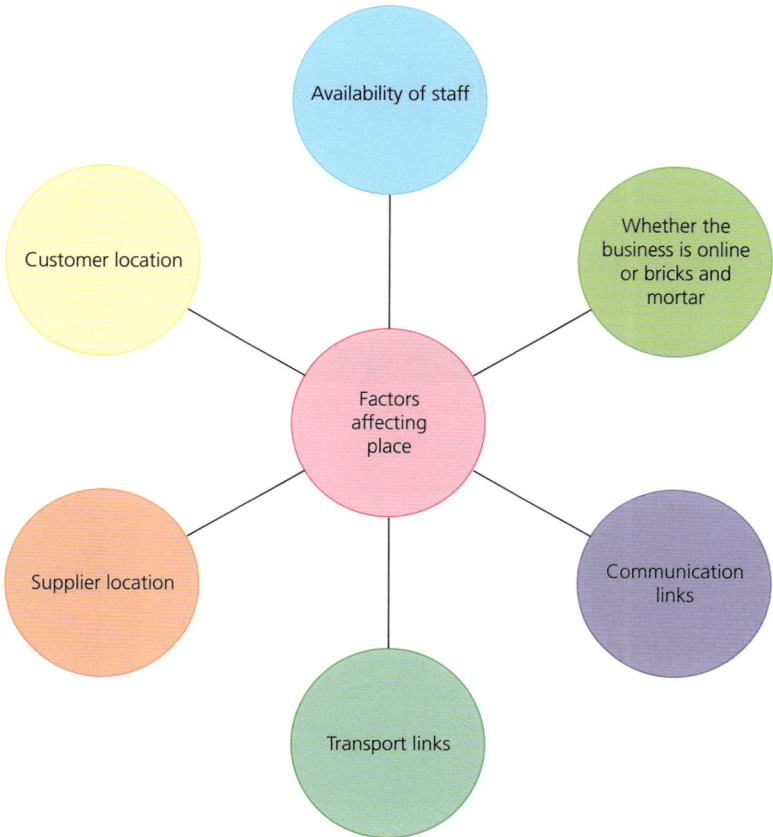

Figure 2.11 Factors affecting place

E-commerce

E-commerce has become increasing popular in recent years. It is a low-cost method of marketing and selling goods. Producers often place their goods on their own website and sell direct to their customers. For customers, e-commerce provides a quick and easy way to purchase goods. There is a risk, however, that the products may not be as they look online, and some consumers are concerned about providing bank or card details to complete purchases online. Amazon is a good example of successful e-commerce. Social media is also a good example of the power of e-commerce, with sales generated by individuals purchasing products that they see on social media platforms.

> ### Activity
> Make a list of products that are sold via each of the following channels of distribution:
> - Retailers
> - Wholesalers
> - Mail order
> - Internet selling (e-commerce)

> ### Test yourself
> 1. Write an explanation of price.
> 2. Write an explanation of place.
> 3. Give three different examples of place.

2.3.3 Promotion

Businesses use a range of different promotional methods to achieve a specific marketing goal. The promotional mix has several different elements.

Promotional methods

Advertising

Businesses may produce advertisements for their products. A business needs to ensure that its advertising focuses on the target audience and the products/services that it is trying to sell.

Table 2.4

Advantages	Disadvantages
A successful advertising campaign can be an effective way of attracting new customers, as well as reminding existing customers how good a product/service is.	Advertising costs can be incredibly high.
Effective advertising has a wide coverage, meaning that a lot of different people will see the advertisement.	There is no guarantee that an advertising campaign will increase sales of the product, so it can be a financially risky strategy.
Businesses have full control of their advertisements, meaning they can make sure the message they send out is the one that they wish to portray.	Advertisements are impersonal, as they are aimed at a wide range of people.
As advertisements are often repeated regularly, the business's message can be effectively communicated and is likely to build brand loyalty.	Advertisements are one-way communication and lack flexibility. They cannot be adjusted and do not allow customers to ask questions.

Print media

Posters

Posters can appear in and on a range of different mediums, including on taxis, buses, billboards and in shops. They need to be eye-catching to attract people's attention.

Advantages:

- Posters can be cheap to produce, but cost depends on the size of the poster and the number of posters required.
- They can be posted in specific areas to attract the target market.
- They are easy to read.
- Well-designed posters are eye-catching.

Disadvantages:

- May be ignored if they are not relevant to the people who see them.
- Posters can have limited impact if the target market consumers do not notice them because they are distracted.

Leaflets

Leaflets tend to be used by small businesses as they are low-cost and can target customers in the local area. For example, fast-food takeaway shops often use leaflets posted through doors to promote their menus.

Advantages:

- Leaflets are relatively cheap to produce and can contain a large amount of information.
- They can target customers in the local area.
- They can be distributed to a wide range of potential customers.
- They are easy to read and have good visual impact.

Disadvantages:

- Leaflets may be thrown away once read.
- They can be seen as junk mail and not read.
- As they are not usually kept, they do not have a long-term impact.

Billboards

Billboards are still a popular form of advertising. A billboard is a large poster that is placed on a display board on the side of a building or bus shelter for people to view. Electronic billboards that display a number of different advertisements are becoming more common.

Advantages:

- This form of advertising is affordable for larger businesses.
- As billboards are large, they can be seen for long distances.

Disadvantages:

- For a small business, this form of advertising will be expensive.

Digital media

Websites

Many businesses choose to advertise their products on websites. Businesses can choose to:

- place adverts on search engine results pages
- pay for pop-ups (small windows that appear over the top of web pages and are used to attract attention)
- place adverts on social media sites.

Social media

Businesses may also have their own accounts on social media platforms such as Facebook or Twitter.

Advantages:

- Adverts on social media are relatively cheap to produce and distribute.
- Social media accounts can be used to update customers on current offers, new products and promotions.
- They have been proved to increase sales.

- Social media allows access to international markets.
- Advertising on social media allows customer feedback to be gained.

Disadvantages:

- Adverts on social media are less useful for businesses that target a market who are less 'tech savvy' and less likely to go online.
- Social media requires daily monitoring to prevent inappropriate behaviour.
- There are risks of negative reviews, information leaks or hacking.

Broadcast media

Promoting a business using TV or radio can help to reach a wide range of audiences.

TV

There are many TV channels and ways of advertising on the different channels, for example, traditional advertisements or programme sponsorship.

Advantages:

- A business can target its advertisements at the selected audience. For example, children's toys could be advertised on a children's TV channel, while a historical magazine could be advertised on the History Channel.
- A national audience can be reached.

Disadvantages:

- It is expensive to create TV advertisements.
- Advertisements can be 'muted' by the audience or ignored, which provides little impact on the chosen audience.

Radio

Businesses tend to use specific radio stations and programmes for their particular target market. For example, a sportswear store may use a football show on its local radio station to advertise its new range of football shirts.

Advantages:

- Use of sounds and music can help radio advertisements attract attention.
- Specific audiences can be targeted by choosing an appropriate station and programme on which to advertise.
- Radio advertisements can be produced very quickly.
- Advertising on radio is considerably cheaper than advertising on TV.

Disadvantages:

- Radios are often used as background noise, so advertisements can be missed or ignored.
- Prime slots in the morning or evening are considerably more expensive than other times during the day.
- There is no way to save an advertisement, so the listener needs to take in all of the information at once.

2 Market research, market types and orientation and marketing mix

> **Activity**
>
> Claret Gym, in Turf Town, has been open for two months. The gym is independently owned and is not part of a national chain. There are several other larger gyms in the town but the customer service at Claret Gym is its unique selling point when attracting customers.
>
> ■ Complete a table like the one below to advise the owners about the most appropriate advertising methods to attract and retain members.
>
> | Advertising method | Description | Advantages | Disadvantages |
> |---|---|---|---|
> | | | | |
> | | | | |
> | | | | |

Sales promotion

Sales promotions are used by businesses to provide a short-term boost to their sales. A number of different techniques can be used, as shown in Figure 2.12.

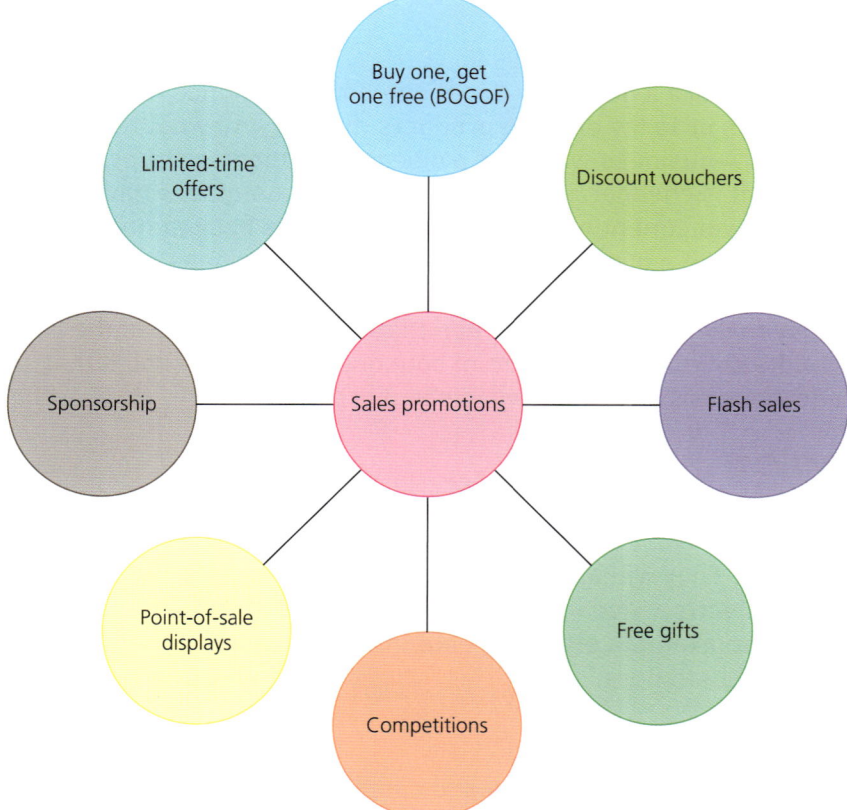

Figure 2.12 Sales promotions

Figure 2.13 Limited-time offers

Businesses always have key objectives when completing any promotional activity. These include:

- increasing consumer knowledge
- increasing market share
- communicating with customers
- encouraging purchasing
- developing customer loyalty.

Limited-time offers

Limited-time offers are a method of achieving a large number of sales in a short time, providing that customers want and need the product. A business will discount a product/service for a short amount of time to encourage customers to purchase it during the offer period.

Buy one, get one free (BOGOF)

Some businesses may offer a buy one, get one free option, also known as a BOGOF. A customer will purchase one item and then be able to get another one for free, meaning that they get two items for the price of one. The disadvantage of BOGOF offers is that they reduce the business's profit margins for the time of the offer period.

Discount vouchers

Discount vouchers are a good way to get customers to notice new products/services or to try existing products that they may not have previously tried. A business will offer a discount on the normal price of the item so that it is cheaper, in the hope that once customers have tried something they will continue to purchase it when it is back at normal price. For example, if a product costs £2.00 and the business offers a 50% discount voucher, the customer would pay just £1.00. The business therefore may make little or no profit on that item for the time of the offer. Discounts could be in the form of coupons or seasonal sales that appear in newspapers and online via discounts websites.

Flash sales

Flash sales are slightly different from limited-time offers as they tend to be for just one or two days. These often appear on websites or social media platforms. They will appear with the intention of creating large sales of the product/service for the 24 or 48 hours that it is on offer. Black Friday is an example of a flash sale that encourages impulse purchases from customers.

Free gifts

Free gifts may be given by businesses to customers who are purchasing items from the business. Products such as aftershave or perfume are associated with such free products as they are expensive to purchase

2 Market research, market types and orientation and marketing mix

and considered to be luxury items. At celebratory times of the year, such as Christmas, customers will often be offered free items such as T-shirts or sweatshirts that advertise the brand, or body lotions or shampoos made by the same business.

The idea of these promotional activities is that the customer may purchase the product/service with a free gift rather than a competitor's product/service now and may continue to buy the promoted product/service when it is no longer on offer.

Other promotional activities include competitions and point-of-sale displays.

Competitions

Competitions might be used by a business to generate sales for products/services, where sales are falling. By advertising a competition on a packet or as part of a service, the customer may be more drawn to buy it, as they could win a prize. For example, when there is a large sporting event happening, such as the Olympics or the football World Cup or Euros, free tickets are given away with purchases of soft drink and snack to competition winners as prizes so that they can attend the most sought-after events, such as finals days.

Point-of-sale displays

Point-of-sale displays promote products near to the tills where a customer will pay for their shopping. Supermarkets are renowned for their point-of-sale promotions and often will have snacks on display to entice customers to purchase the items just as they are about to pay for the rest of their shopping.

Case study

Businesses came under fire when research was completed into the types of items that were often stocked near supermarket tills. The obesity levels of the UK population are increasing, and most point-of-sale displays are convenience snack foods such as chocolate, crisps and fizzy drinks. Businesses with point-of-sale displays received negative press. The celebrity chef Hugh Fearnley-Whittingstall investigated this specifically at WHSmith and, over time, he was able to influence businesses to re-think their point-of-sale advertising, focusing on more healthy snacks for customers to purchase.

Watch the following clip: https://www.dailymail.co.uk/femail/article-5648821/Hugh-Fearnley-Whittingstall-wages-war-WHSmith.html

Answer the following questions:
1. What are your thoughts on the video clip?
2. When was the last time you purchased an item at the tills, and what was it?
3. Did you specifically go to the till to purchase it as you knew it would be there, or did you buy it because you saw the item and wanted it as an impulse purchase?
4. What else have you purchased because you saw it, but which you had not gone specifically into the shop to purchase?
5. What do you see as the key themes from this video clip?

Loyalty schemes

Loyalty schemes allow the consumer to gain points every time they purchase products from the business. Building up points leads to money off shopping or money off leisure activities. Such schemes enable the business to build up consumer profiles, for example by recording their average monthly spend and the types of products/services bought. This means that the business can target certain products at consumers by enticing them with money-off coupons or other sales promotions, to get them to purchase a particular brand. The system works because consumers feel that they are getting value for money and will therefore keep purchasing to collect points.

Case study

Figure 2.14 Green Shield stamps were the first loyalty scheme

Loyalty cards benefit both consumers and businesses. The concept started many years ago when the founder of the Green Shield stamps loyalty scheme, Richard Tompkins, heard of a similar idea that was being used successfully in America. With Green Shield, shoppers received one stamp for every 6p they spent on shopping, which they could then use for credit in one of the shops taking part in the scheme, or use the stamps to order products from a catalogue. The scheme ran from 1958 to 1991. Tesco launched its very successful Clubcard in the mid-1990s, which continues today. Other successful loyalty cards are Sainsbury's Nectar card and the Boots Advantage Card.

Answer the following questions:

1 Write a list of five different loyalty card schemes (not those from the above case study), stating the name of the card and which business it is associated with.
2 Select two different cards and investigate how many points you get per £1 that you spend. How much do you need to spend to gain either a substantial amount (£10) of money off or a free item, for example a coffee in a coffee shop?
3 Consider the results that you have found. Do the figures surprise you in any way? Do you think that the loyalty cards are worth using? Explain your answer.
4 Prepare a table that compares and contrasts the features of each loyalty card scheme. Write a paragraph to explain which one most attracts you as a customer.

Sponsorship

Sponsorship is another method of promotion for a business's brand. Examples include placing the name of a business on a sports team's shirts or sponsoring (financially supporting) a large community event. By sponsoring an event, the business's name will be displayed on merchandise associated with the event or it will be mentioned by a presenter covering the event. Television programmes can also be sponsored by a brand, meaning that any advertisement breaks will feature the brand's products.

2 Market research, market types and orientation and marketing mix

Direct marketing

Direct marketing is when businesses sell products/services directly to the public rather than selling via a retailer. They may use mail order, online or telephone sales techniques.

Emails

Emails can be sent directly to customers and potential customers who are on a mailing list that a business has compiled or bought. A business can use this form of sales promotion to promote a new product/service, special offers or to give notice of a sale that may interest the customer. The email could include a special discount code. A business will use these activities to encourage engagement with customers and increase sales of its products/services. However, businesses will need to follow data protection legislation (see Section 7.1.1 for more details of this).

Figure 2.15 Sponsorship

Advantages:

- Emails can be targeted at specific customers, which will include existing and potential customers.
- They are quick to send.
- They can be sent around the world.

Disadvantages:

- It is hard for a business to measure the impact of an email.
- They can be ignored by the recipient.
- They may be marked as spam and so not get read.

Flyers

Flyers enable a business to advertise its products/services to potential customers. They are displayed in prominent places where customers will be drawn to look at them, sent in the post or put through people's front doors. It is a popular method of marketing for takeaway food businesses as they can display their menus and provide incentives for the service that they offer. Flyers can be similar to leaflets (see page 51).

Advantages:

- Visual appeal to the reader.
- Can be designed how the creator wants.
- Can be targeted to a specific audience, e.g. customers who read a specific magazine.

Disadvantages:

- Expensive to produce.
- They are often ignored and put in the recycling bin without being read.

SMS texts

SMS refers to a 'Short Message Service' that sends text messages to mobile phones. Over the years, businesses have realised that this can be used as a form of advertising, as texts are sent directly to the registered user of the mobile phone.

57

Advantages:

- Texts have a high reader rate, as they are short and sent directly to the user's mobile phone.
- They are quick and easy to create.
- They are a reliable form of advertising for the sender.
- They can be stopped if the user texts the business directly.

Disadvantages:

- The messages are short so misunderstandings can occur.
- Limited information can be given in a text.
- They are impersonal.
- They can be distracting for the user of the mobile phone, which therefore can cause a nuisance.

Social media

The use of social media such as Facebook and Twitter to advertise products and gather feedback is a rapidly growing area for many businesses.

Social media advertising can be business-generated, meaning that a business creates a social media page for its business, informing the audience directly about itself and its products/services. Social media can also enable a business to advertise its products/services in the feed of individual users. The user may be drawn to its products and click on a link to the business's website to explore further. See pages 51-52 for the advantages and disadvantages of social media.

Factors that influence the promotional mix

There are many different ways that a business can encourage customer engagement through using the methods known as the promotional mix. There are a number of different factors that might influence the promotional mix that a business chooses to use, shown in Figure 2.16.

Target market	The nature of the market	Finance available	Competitor mix	The nature of the product/service
A business must be clear who its products are aimed at so that its marketing will appeal to the specific audience	It is important for the business to understand the market that it is operating within, which will include the peaks and lows of sales	A business must be clear who its products are aimed at so that its finance options will appeal to the specific audience	A business must be aware of the activities of its competitors, which may change. The business must have a clear plan for its own marketing activities to retain its customers	Businesses may need to be inventive with their promotional methods and alter their activities according to products/services that they are selling

Figure 2.16 Factors that influence the promotional mix

2 Market research, market types and orientation and marketing mix

Promotional objectives

Having clear objectives will help a business determine what it is striving to achieve with its promotional activities. The most common forms of promotional objectives for a business can be seen in Figure 2.17.

Figure 2.17 Promotional objectives

If a business achieves these four promotional objectives, it will be in a better market position to have continued success in the future.

Test yourself

1. Explain the difference between price skimming and penetration pricing.
2. What are the four key elements of promotion?
3. Write a definition of a sales promotion.
4. Explain two advantages of a business producing a poster as part of an advertising campaign.
5. Identify a flash sale activity that a business may use.
6. Identify and describe three advertising methods that could be used by a clothing retailer.
7. Identify and describe three sales promotion techniques.

NCFE Level 1/2 Technical Award in Business and Enterprise

2.3.4 Product

Having a suitable product/service for a business is an important part of the marketing mix. If customers do not want or need a product/service, sales will not be made.

A business should focus on four key areas when devising its product ideas:

- Unique selling point (USP)
- Needs of the target market
- Brand image
- Product quality

Activity

In pairs, think of ten different brands covering a range of different products, to include technology, food, soft drinks and household items. Write a description of each brand and include clues to enable a person reading the description to identify the brand being described. An example is below:

- Description: A well-known technology brand that has a link to a fruit.
- Answer: Apple

USP

All businesses try to find their product's major strength, which they can refer to as its USP. Making sure that a product 'stands out' above others is the key to making a sale. USPs of products/services may include the quality of the materials used to make it, the selling price, the variety of colours available or where it can be bought.

The benefits of developing a new product are that the business can:

- invent a product with a specific USP
- promote the strengths of the new product
- increase sales of this new product.

The risks of developing a new product are:

- it takes time and money to establish a new product
- if customers do not want or need the product, it will not sell
- there is a risk of losing money if limited sales are made.

Activity

Think of four different businesses — one that produces a drink, one related to food, one producing technological products and one that specialises in holidays.

- Copy and complete the following table.

Type of business	Name of business	Name of product/service	USP
Drinks company			
Food company			
Technology company			
Holiday company			

- Use the internet to research the different types of advertisements used for products similar to those in your table.
- Using this information, select one of the businesses from your table and produce an advertisement that highlights the USP of its product/service, to try and persuade customers to purchase it.

2 Market research, market types and orientation and marketing mix

The needs of the target market

Producing a product/service that is wanted and needed by the target market is vital to the success of a business enterprise. We are all individuals and we all have different tastes, so what appeals to you may not appeal to someone else. That is why businesses need to know what their customers will purchase, which relates to **customer profiling**. Therefore, understanding the needs of the target market is also very important. A business can do this by listing all the different needs of its customers, which can be identified by asking questions about them to build up a picture of those customers. Questions could be: Are they male or female? Do they have children? Do they play sport? What is their average annual income? The answers to these questions will enable the business to work out the needs and wants of its target market.

Brand image

A brand is how a business can be identified. A brand is not just its name, but how customers regard the business as a whole. If a brand is successful, then customers learn to trust the brand and will purchase any new products produced under that brand. A brand can be recognised from a famous phrase, an image or a particular identity. Think about the activity that you completed at the start of this section: those brands are famous and most will have been around for several years or even decades.

So how does a business come up with a brand? Before a business can develop a brand, it first needs to consider the following elements:

- Brand personality — A brand personality takes time to establish develop them, just like we develop our personalities over time. Businesses have to consider a range of different elements to ensure that the brand personality meets the requirements of their customers. If sales are declining, businesses can also re-invent brands by re-launching them in a different way. For example, Apple first started producing desktop computers but then changed when it extended its brand with the iPhone and iPad.
- Brand identity — The identify of a brand is the visual elements that identify the brand from others that are similar in the market, and also the perception of the product from its customers when using it. For example, look at Figure 2.18. What business is associated with this colour? This demonstrates the power of just a colour on a brand image.
- Brand name — Brand names are the names that a business uses to identify the portfolio of products that it produces. Some brands have a whole range of products, while others may only have two or three that customers can purchase. Think of Warburtons, which is famous for producing bread. Did you also know that it produces bagels, muffins, potato cakes, crumpets, tea cakes, fruit loaves and pancakes? That is so much more than just bread!

(For more on brand image, see Section 2.3.8.)

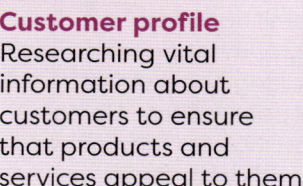

Key term

Customer profile Researching vital information about customers to ensure that products and services appeal to them.

Figure 2.18 What business is associated with this colour?

Activity

Research the products that the following brands produce:
- Colgate
- Daewoo
- Walkers.

NCFE Level 1/2 Technical Award in Business and Enterprise

Activity

Kamil has been experimenting with making items out of wooden pallets. He has had interest from a few friends with the items that he has made so far. He has decided to start a new business using wooden pallets and wants to create a typeface and logo for his brand.

Look at the following websites and write a short guide for Kamil.

- www.business2community.com/branding/15-of-the-best-business-fonts-to-use-for-your-logo-02296761
- www.creativebloq.com/graphic-design/pro-guide-logo-design-21221

Product quality

Quality is an important aspect for any business. It is important for a business to produce a product/service that is of good quality so that repeat sales can occur. Businesses need to check that their products and services meet the required standards so that customers will be satisfied. For example, imagine if you purchased your favourite chocolate bar, and it did not taste the same as it normally does. Businesses must therefore understand the importance of producing high-quality products/services for their customers.

The advantages of ensuring that the business produces high-quality products include:

- The business will gain a good reputation for producing quality products/services.
- Repeat custom will increase due to the business's positive reputation.
- Word will spread about the quality of its products, so attracting new customers.

The disadvantages for the business include:

- The business will have to invest time into producing high-quality products.
- Money will need to be spent to ensure that the products/services meet the required quality control checks so that customers can be guaranteed quality products.
- If the quality checks fail, customers may need to be compensated, which would impact on the business's profits as well as damage its reputation.

(For more on maintaining quality, see Section 4.1.3.)

Case study

Case study 1

Perrier is famous for its sparkling water, but in 1990 impurities were discovered in some bottles. The impurity was a toxic substance called benzine. Within one week of the findings, the company decided to recall 160 million bottles of water. The company subsequently discovered that the toxic substance had been caused by human error due to filters that had not been changed at the bottling plant. Move forward to 2022 and Perrier is now available in 140 countries worldwide and sells over 1 billion products a year.

2 Market research, market types and orientation and marketing mix

Case study 2

In 2018, BMW was forced to recall more than 300,000 cars in the UK because it had been reported that the engines in some cars were cutting out due to an electrical fault. It contacted customers who had purchased specific cars between March 2007 and August 2011. An investigation by the BBC's *Watchdog* programme highlighted several customers whose BMW car engine had cut out while driving. BMW was also criticised for failing to tell the Driver and Vehicle Standards Agency of the electrical failure in its cars between 2001 and 2014, as it was required to do.

Answer the following questions:
1 Identify the main points made in the two case studies.
2 How do you think that these brands were damaged as a result of these investigations into product quality?
3 What would you advise the businesses to do to ensure that errors like these do not occur again?

Test yourself

1 Which of the four 4Ps is most important?
2 Identify the four main elements that a business needs to consider related to a product.
3 Write a definition of 'brand image'.
4 What method could a business adopt to identify the needs of their target market?
5 Why is it important for a business to produce quality products/services?

2.3.5 Product life cycle and product life cycle extension strategies

Product life cycle

All products have a unique **product life cycle** that shows the stages a product goes through from its introduction and launch until it is removed from sale. Some products naturally decline in popularity, while some never succeed; a few will continue to grow and survive in the market for many years.

Stages and characteristics

There are four main stages that generally occur in the product life cycle, as shown in Table 2.4.

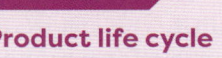

Key term

Product life cycle
Traces the journey of a product from its development and launch to its removal from sale to the public.

NCFE Level 1/2 Technical Award in Business and Enterprise

Table 2.4 Description of the stages of the product life cycle

Life cycle stage	Description
1: Introduction	This is when a business launches the new product onto the market and makes it available for sale. The business advertises the product heavily during this stage in order to improve customer awareness of the product and encourage sales. At this stage, the company will be making low profits or possibly losing money and will have a low market share.
2: Growth	During this stage of the life cycle, customers are familiar with the product and sales are increasing. The number of sales increases at its fastest rate and profits rise. Competitors may enter the market if the product is a success.
3: Maturity	During this stage, sales of the product have reached their highest level. It is likely that the number of new customers is reducing and growth is limited. Other businesses may have entered the market to compete or the number of products available may mean the market is saturated. The business will work hard to promote their product to maintain their market share.
4: Decline	In the decline phase, sales of the product begin to fall. Customers are no longer interested in the product and may have switched to newer alternative products. The business does not actively promote the product and eventually removes it from sale.

A product life cycle is usually represented on a graph like the one in Figure 2.19.

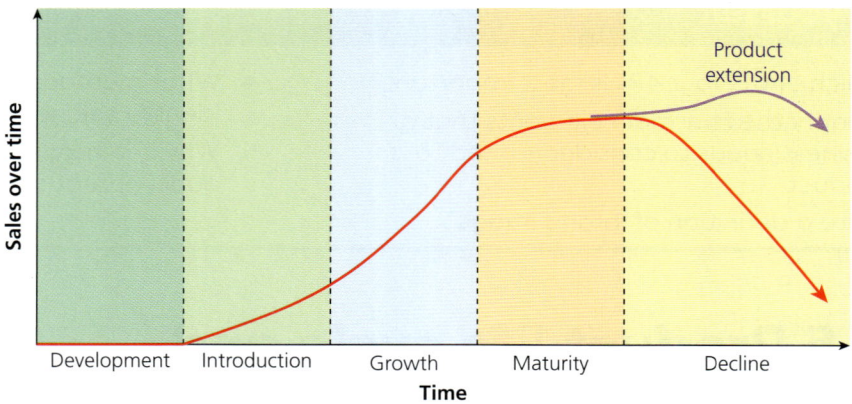

Figure 2.19 The product life cycle

Activity

- Copy and label the product life cycle diagram.
- Identify the stages of a product life cycle for a mobile phone.
- In pairs, discuss how long each of the different stages may be and when the manufacturer is likely to introduce a new model.

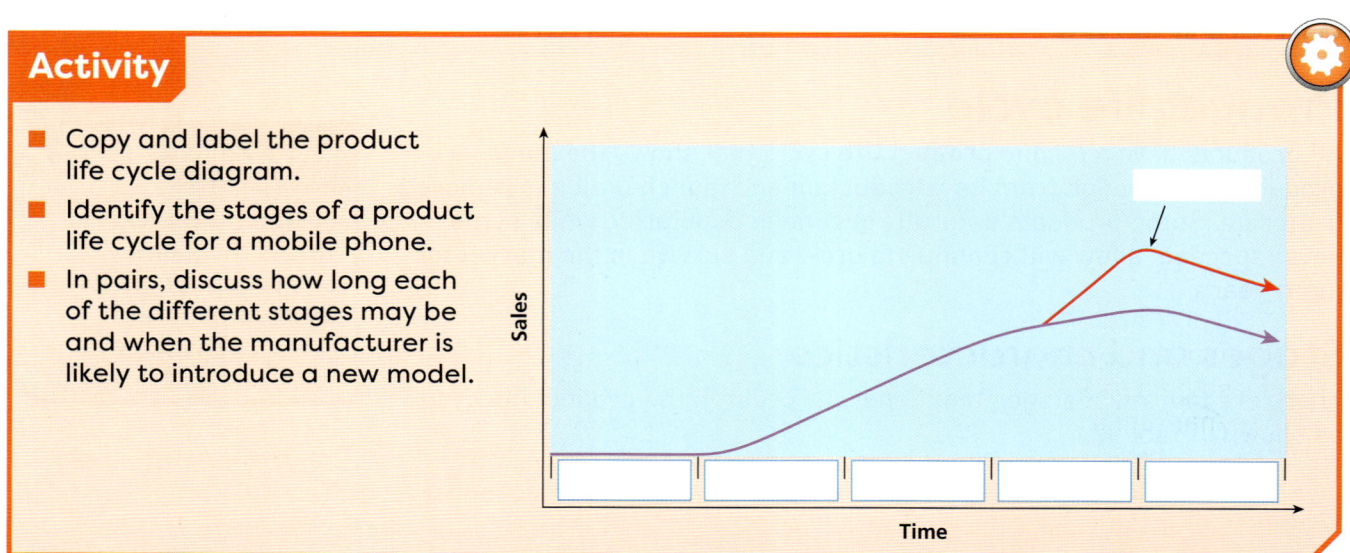

Product life cycle extension strategies

It is often cheaper for a business to make changes to a current product than to develop a brand, new product. With this in mind, businesses may try to extend the life (the growth and maturity phases) of successful products using extension strategies.

Changes in the marketing mix

There are a number of different strategies that a business can use to extend the life of a product:

- New advertising campaigns — Aim to attract both new and existing customers. (For more on advertising, see Section 2.3.3 on promotion.)
- New pricing strategies — Reducing the selling price of products and services give customers more value for money. (For more on pricing strategies, see Section 2.3.1 on pricing.)
- New product features — A business will often want to add extra features and functions to their products and stores to increase sales. For example, drive-through facilities, table service and/or the option to order on screen are popular at fast food outlets. Depending on what is required, changes to location, features and functions may be expensive to implement and so would reduce profits for the business.

New packaging is often a relatively cheap method of updating a product, by changing the colours or logos. If a business provides improved packaging, customers may perceive an increase in quality and therefore be prepared to pay a higher price.

A business may decide to increase or reduce the price of its product.

Increasing the price makes more revenue and therefore more profit for a business. Raising the price alongside a re-branding of the product may allow a business to enter the 'luxury' market. In this market, people are prepared to pay more for products, therefore increasing profit.

The disadvantages of increasing the product price are that it may mean customers buy products from competitors who may offer a cheaper price. An increase in product price is also likely to mean that customers expect a better quality product.

Adding value is a popular strategy to extend the life of a product. This involves the business adding new features to an existing product. For example, adding extra memory or a better camera or screen to a mobile phone, or creating a cordless version of a vacuum cleaner. This strategy works well for brands that are well known and have been popular for many years. By adding value, businesses can charge customers more for their products.

Re-launching an existing product can be costly, however, and requires considerable financial investment in terms of research, piloting, trialling and then marketing the updated product. Adding value will not be successful if there is no demand for the original product. Therefore, before adding value, a business needs to check that there is likely to still be demand for the product in the future.

Figure 2.20 A product with added value: the Dyson V8 cordless vacuum cleaner

NCFE Level 1/2 Technical Award in Business and Enterprise

Entering new markets

This is when a business has the opportunity to enter a new market where there isn't existing demand, but there could be. It is a risk, but could have a large pay-off. Therefore, it is important for the business to know how, why and when to enter a new market.

How to enter a new market

Creating a profile of the potential customers in the new market will enable the business to work out the different elements that it will need to consider. A customer profile will involve the business researching the customers — their gender, lifestyle, income, profession, etc. It is important that the business establishes that there is a need for the product or service and researches why customers have this need, to ensure that it isn't already being met elsewhere by a competitor. The business will also need to plan the timeframe for entering the new market to ensure that the product has maximum impact, for example for a seasonal product.

Why enter a new market?

The most important reason to consider entering a new market is that the business could end up with new customers, thus increasing sales and profits for the business. It will enable the business to diversify into new markets. This enables the business to make new choices and create new opportunities. This can bring life back into the business and create a 'buzz', but it is important that the new markets are well researched.

When to enter a new market

Providing he business has completed thorough research for how and why the it is entering a new market, the last area that needs to be considered is when this will all happen. A business would be advised to create a plan known as a strategy, so that there is focus for the business. The strategy should contain information on:

- The overall plan, which details the promotions/campaigns as well as timelines for these to be set in motion.
- Clear communication to the relevant individuals within the business of the planned activities to ensure success.
- An exit strategy, which means the business has prepared for both success and failure. If failure does occur, the business should know when and where to stop. This is to ensure that the brand image is not damaged for the other products that it produces.

Activity

James Dyson became famous for inventing a new style vacuum cleaner, but did you know he has also produced other products?

- Research these products and produce a poster that advertises the range of Dyson products that can be purchased.

Read about it

www.americanexpress.com/en-us/business/trends-and-insights/articles/usp-101-how-to-uncover-your-unique-selling-proposition — Advice on finding your USP.

Test yourself

1. What does USP stand for?
2. How many parts are there in the product life cycle?
3. What are the different stages of the product life cycle?
4. Explain one method that a business could use to extend the life of a product.
5. What can a business do to enter a new market?

2 Market research, market types and orientation and marketing mix

2.3.6 Product development and innovation

To be successful and remain competitive, a business must continually create new products/services or update existing ones which satisfy its customers changing needs and wants. It will need to use **innovation** to generate these new ideas. Once an idea has been selected, **Product development**, which is the process of bringing a product from an idea through to launching it into the market, can begin.

- Remaining competitive — New product development should allow a business to keep existing and attract new customers. This means that it will remain competitive and be able to compete with its rivals in the market. Without new products, customers will move to other providers.
- Entering new markets — If a business is selling a product that has universal appeal but has yet to target a full range of customers, then it could investigate offering the product for sale in new areas. This could include introducing a children's range of an adult product or starting to sell in different areas of the country.
- Increasing market share — New products enable a business to diversify and enter new markets. This will mean that it has the opportunity to increase its market share and also increase its sales.

In cases where a business needs to differentiate itself further, it may decide to make improvements to its current product offering. Changes it may consider making include:

- Altering the product's location — This could be the location of a product in a particular store or the geographical location where a product is sold.
- Altering the product's features and functions — For example, a supermarket may increase the number of its stores that have a café or a pharmacy.
- Altering the product's design and appearance — Many products have packaging 'face lifts' to increase their appeal.

If a business can successfully tap into a new market, it may see its sales, and therefore its profits, increase considerably. This strategy may not be suitable for every product, however. Certain products may only be popular in certain geographic locations, for example, kilts may be popular in Scotland but have a limited market in Wales.

> **Key terms**
>
> **Innovation** A new idea or method, or the process of using new ideas and methods.
>
> **Product development** The processes of bringing a product from being a concept through to reaching the market.

Figure 2.21 H&M is an existing brand that has adapted its products and processes to appeal to a broader target audience

> **Activity**
>
> Consider the technology industry and select a product of your choice, for example a games console, computer or mobile phone.
> - In small groups, discuss the different extension strategies that have been used to extend the life of your chosen product.

NCFE Level 1/2 Technical Award in Business and Enterprise

Activity

In recent years, there has been an increased amount of competition among food retailers. Consider the supermarkets in your local area.

- In small groups, discuss how the supermarkets have adapted and improved their offering in order to compete with one another.

Case study

Ryder Golf and Sports Equipment developed a 'fitness band', called Golf IT, ten years ago. This equipment is worn by golfers to record how far they have walked around the golf course. In the last two years, the business has seen very little sales growth and, in the last six months, sales have started to decline.

Answer the following questions:

1. Consider what extension strategies Ryder Golf and Sports Equipment could use to extend the life of Golf IT.
2. Review the advantages and disadvantages of each of the strategies suggested.

Comply with changes in legislation

A business may need to develop an existing product due to changes in government legislation. If the law changes, the business must comply with the new rules. For example, in July 2021 the government introduced a new law that legally required manufacturers of electrical appliances to produce spareparts for their customers. The new rules were introduced to extend the lifespan of these products in order to benefit the environment (source: www.bbc.co.uk/news/business-57665593).

Produce patents

If a business creates a new and unique product/service, it can patent it. A **patent** is a licence that gives the holder of it the exclusive right for a set time to produce and sell the patented product and to exclude others from making, using or selling the invention. This means the original inventor can take advantage of the increasing sales of the product before competitors try to produce something similar, remembering of course that these cannot be exactly the same!

Key term

Patent A licence that gives the holder the exclusive right for a set time to produce and sell the patented product and to exclude others from making, using or selling the invention.

Case study

Connor enjoyed producing a homemade lemonade drink that his great-grandmother taught him how to make using a special family recipe. However, trying to keep the lemonade fresh was hard using the limited materials he had. So, he spent time using technology to produce a special type of bottle that would increase the shelf-life of the product. It involved using a unique processing method and a new type of seal on the bottles. This now means that the product does not need to be stored at a cold temperature before the seal is broken. He is hoping that his great-grandmother's homemade lemonade can now be enjoyed by many more people.

Answer the following questions:

1. Why might Connor decide to patent the new type of bottle with a special seal for the lemonade?
2. How would having a patent help Connor with this new technological design?

2 Market research, market types and orientation and marketing mix

2.3.7 Boston Matrix

The Boston Matrix is a way of analysing the product portfolio (the range of different products/services) offered for sale by a business. Businesses categorise their products into one of four categories.

- Stars — These are products that have a high market share in a fast-growing market. Once R&D costs have been recouped, these will be starting to generate profit for the business and will ensure it remains competitive.
- Question marks — These are products that have a low market share in a fast-growing market. These will be a cause for concern for the business owners and may need to be retired. They can be referred to as 'problem children'.
- Cash cows — These are products that have a high market share in a slow-growing market. They tend to be highly successful products that stay in the market for many years. These will generate most profit for the business.
- Dogs — These are products that have a low market share in a slow-growing market. These will generate little or no profit so business owners will often remove these products from the market, unless they are needed to ensure sales of another, more successful, product.

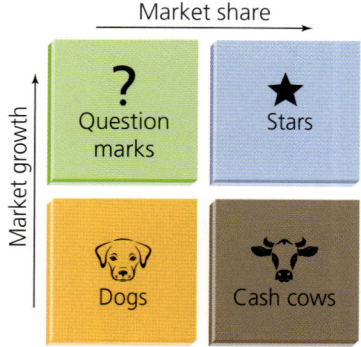

Figure 2.22 The Boston Matrix

Activity

In pairs, think about products that you remember purchasing a few years ago that now are not available. Research when these products were withdrawn and think about why they were discontinued. Feed back your findings back to the rest of the class.

If a business has only a few products in its range and these are all in the same category, it is important that it tries to extend its product range to include more stars which will hopefully become cash cows in the future.

Uses of the Boston Matrix

A business will use the Boston Matrix to help determine several factors:

- Product classification — To review its products to determine if they are still current and therefore worth producing, using market share and rate of growth figures. The business must not become complacent in its approach and should remain informed about the performance of all its products/services.
- Product portfolio decisions — The decisions could focus on the value of each product in the portfolio and determine which ones require more publicity to increase customer awareness to generate more sales.
- Product withdrawal — This is when a business reviews its product portfolio and determines which products are performing the best and the worst. It will then have to discuss which ones may potentially be withdrawn, meaning that they will no longer be produced.
- Product development — If a portfolio has only cash cows, which may age to be dogs and no (or few) stars, the business must aim to develop new products that will hopefully become stars (rather than question marks).

69

2.3.8 Branding

A brand is how a business is identified by others, such as its customers as well as its competitors.

Section 2.3.4 explained how important it is for a business to establish a brand image. It can then use the brand for promotion and to introduce new products to its existing customers to generate more sales and increase its market share. This all starts with creating a strong brand image.

Brand image

Famous brands are recognised in various forms, whether by name, logo, font or colour used. Having a clear brand means loyal customers can easily identify and purchase other, new products/services from the same brand because they trust it and know what to expect from the brand.

Many brand images are quite simple yet have a strong presence. A simple and bold design may be the most easily recognised by consumers.

Brand image can include the visual elements of a logo, but there is more to a brand image than just a symbol, sign or logo.

- Reputation and trust — Branding is important to a business, as it forms an important part of its reputation. If a business has a good reputation, customers will talk about it in a positive way to others, who might then purchase the brand's products/services. However, if the brand's reputation is negative, this may put off potential customers, which will ultimately mean that customers are lost, leading to a reduction in profits. A business's reputation can be damaged by one single event. A company can then have to spend a great deal of time and money re-building its damaged brand. Sometimes this works, but often it does not. (See, for example, the case studies on Perrier and BMW in Section 2.3.4.)
- Quality — Brand image involves quality. If you purchase a product and it breaks within the first week, your view of the company that produced it may change. If you take the product back and exchange it for the same model and it breaks again, would you take it back and replace it again or would you ask for a refund? A business does not want to gain a reputation for producing poor quality goods or providing poor service, as customers will make their views known. People often post a review of items or of the company itself on the business's website or rate products online. Online reviews can therefore be a good gauge as to whether or not a product you are thinking of buying is a quality item. For more on quality, see Section 2.3.4.
- Can allow for setting higher prices — Most customers want 'value for money': they want to feel the amount of money they paid for the item reflects its actual worth. Sometimes customers are happy to spend a little more if they feel this means they will get a better quality product. If a business develops a brand image that is linked to high quality, they can charge higher prices for their products/services.

2 Market research, market types and orientation and marketing mix

- Lifestyle — Particular products and services are aimed at a certain lifestyle based on customer profiles. Therefore, the brand image must be suitable for the business's customer profile. For example, perfumes are luxury, high-price products so their branding is designed to look expensive and luxurious - think about the use of gold, black, smoky glass bottles, etc.
- Develop customer loyalty — Happy and satisfied customers are important to a business as their views can have a strong impact on others. Customer loyalty to a specific brand may last a lifetime, meaning that they will purchase the business's products for many years and will not purchase other brands. An example of this would be a customer who purchases Hovis Granary Thick Sliced Bread every week and will not swap to another brand.

Case study

For many years, the car company Skoda was ridiculed by the motoring industry for producing cars that people did not want. Then Skoda was taken over by Volkswagen (VW), which paved the way for changes: new designs were introduced and the cars became more reliable, modern and relevant. This in turn led to happy customers and a successful and profitable company.

Answer the following question:
1 What conclusions can you draw about successful re-branding from this case study about Skoda?

Brand loyalty

Having a successful and reliable brand helps a business to increase customer loyalty. For example, you may have a particular type of shampoo or toothpaste that you always buy; if this is the case, then you are loyal to that brand and will be regarded as a loyal customer.

Many businesses want to increase the number of loyal customers they have, but this is hard to do, especially when people want value for money. In the past, people would be more loyal to a particular branded product, but the increase in value products in shops has meant customer loyalty is decreasing and can be difficult for a business to maintain. For example, customers may purchase a supermarket own brand that looks similar to a branded product. However, some businesses continue to enjoy a very loyal following even if their products are expensive — a good example of this is Apple.

Businesses can take advantage of brand loyalty when launching new products. They do this by involving loyal customers, making sure they have access to loyalty benefits such as being the first to be able to purchase new products or receiving money-off vouchers or codes so that the new products they launch are an instant success.

Customer loyalty can also be maintained by the service that a customer receives when purchasing a product/service. Many businesses undertake surveys to measure customer satisfaction. When a problem occurs with a product, if a business deals with the customer in a professional way and resolves the issue, this will help to ensure they remain loyal and likely to make future purchases.

Case study

An investigation found that many supermarkets were selling standard own-label products that were identical to their value ranges. Investigators looked at the ingredients and nutritional values of a number of products across two price tiers — standard and value — and concluded that in many cases there was almost no appreciable difference between the two. In some cases, the two versions of the product were even produced in the same factory. The only difference between them was their packaging and, of course, the price being charged. The investigators looked at a range of products including cheddar cheese, corned beef, long-life milk and clear honey. Price variations between the budget and standard versions of the identical products ranged from 25p to 50p, which may not seem much but when added up could make a significant difference to a weekly shopping bill.

Answer the following questions:

1 What are your thoughts about this investigation into brands?
2 Are there certain products that you think do taste different from supermarket own brands? Would you swap?
3 What brands are you loyal to?
4 Make some notes, then discuss with the class whether you think this will affect the products that you will purchase in the future, and why.

Remember

- The marketing mix is the different factors that can be controlled by a business in an attempt to influence customers to purchase its products.
- The marketing mix is known as the 4 Ps — product, price, place, promotion.
- There are four key parts to the product life cycle — introduction, growth, maturity and decline.
- An extension strategy is used to extend the life of an existing product.
- The Boston Matrix is a way of analysing the product portfolio offered for sale by a business.
- The Boston Matrix divides an organisation's products into stars, question marks, cash cows and dogs.
- Brand image enables a business to develop customer loyalty.
- Brand loyalty can help a business to launch new products.

Test yourself

1 What are the four different elements of the Boston Matrix?
2 How can a brand image help a business?

2 Market research, market types and orientation and marketing mix

Practice questions

1. Select which **one** of these is an example of primary research. [1 mark]
   a Newspapers
   b Focus groups
   c Trade magazines
   d Competitor's data

2. Select which **one** of these is an example of secondary market research. [1 mark]
   a Census data
   b Questionnaires
   c Face-to-face interviews
   d Observations

3. Select which **one** of these is a feature of a mass market. [1 mark]
   a Specialised products
   b High sales volume
   c High profit margins
   d Aimed at a small section of the market

4. Select which **one** of these is an example of digital advertising. [1 mark]
   a Radio
   b Cinema
   c Leaflets
   d Websites

5. Select which **one** of the following is **not** one of the 4 Ps. [1 mark]
   a Product
   b Price
   c Placement
   d Promotion

6. What are the many differences between qualitative and quantitative data? [4 marks]

7. Identify **two** key features of a niche market. [2 marks]

8. When a business first starts, sales promotions are sometimes offered. Explain what a sales promotion is. [2 marks]

Answer the following questions using the information below:

Ollie owns a fruit and vegetable market stall. He has been very successful over the past three years and has built up a large and loyal customer base, which has increased each year by 10 per cent. During the pandemic, he noticed that some regular customers were not buying from the stall. He decided he would deliver any leftover stock to these local customers. They were always grateful for the fresh fruit and vegetables.

9. Ollie has been successful for three years and is always looking for new opportunities for his business. Explain where on the product life cycle you think Ollie would be and why. [3 marks]

10. Label and illustrate Ollie's three years of success with his fruit and veg business on the graph below. [4 marks]

11. Ollie recognises the importance of introducing new products to his business. Explain **one** extension strategy that he could use. [2 marks]

12. Ollie and Jasper decide to go into business providing fruit and veg boxes. They will offer six different boxes:
    - Small ordinary box
    - Medium ordinary box
    - Large ordinary box
    - Small organic box
    - Medium organic box
    - Large organic box

NCFE Level 1/2 Technical Award in Business and Enterprise

Discuss whether Ollie and Jasper should introduce psychological pricing or competitive pricing strategies when first starting their business. Your recommendation should include:

- An advantage and disadvantage of using psychological pricing.
- An advantage and disadvantage of using competitive pricing.
- A justification for your decision. [9 marks]

Assignment practice

You have had the idea of starting a sandwich and panini delivery service for companies based in business parks on the outskirts of your town. However, since the pandemic, when many people worked from home, there have been fewer people working in the business park. You wonder how you could therefore make this business idea work. You realise that there may be a market for your business but need to complete some research to ensure that you do not waste your time and money investing in the business idea while the world is learning to live with Covid-19.

Tasks:

1. Decide the methods of research that you should complete and explain, with reasons, the different choices that you have made. (AO1, AO2)

2. Create a questionniare as a method of research. Give the questionniare to five people and analyse the responses. (AO1, AO2, AO3, AO4)

3. You need to calculate the costs of producing your products. Do some secondary research to help you cost out the products that you could sell as part of your sandwich and panini delivery service. Present your findings in a suitable document. (AO1, AO2, AO3, AO4)

4. Using your secondary research from Task 3, decide on the price of your products. Think about different promotions that you could offer your customers and design two examples of promotional materials. Decide which promotional material you will use and why. (AO2, AO4, AO5)

3 Human resource requirements for business and enterprise

About this content area

This content area focuses on the human resource requirements for business and enterprise. You will learn about:

- Human resources — The methods of recruitment that businesses use, the various stages of the recruitment process and the types of employment contracts that can be issued.
- Staff development and monitoring — The various ways of developing staff and monitoring their work activities to ensure that they meet the demands of the business.
- Motivation — How various activities within the business motivate staff to work hard, including financial or non-financial motivational methods.

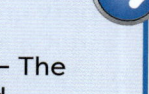

3.1 Human resources

3.1.1 Methods of recruitment

When a new job role is identified or a vacancy is created by a promotion or because an employee leaves the business, it is important that the person who is recruited to fill the position has the right skills, experience and qualifications for the job. A business may decide to advertise a job role within the company (**internal recruitment**) or it may seek to find someone from outside the organisation (**external recruitment**). It could use a combination of the two to get a wider range of applicants.

Internal recruitment

Internal recruitment is when a business seeks to fill a role by recruiting someone who already works at the company. It may do this because there is someone within the organisation who it wants to promote. Internal recruitment means that the successful applicant will already know how the business operates and will understand the systems used. They can therefore settle into the role more quickly than someone from outside, who would need to learn new systems and ways of working. In this way, internal recruitment saves the business time and money. An internal candidate may not know the specific job role and will still need training, but they will already know more about aspects of the business than someone who is new to the organisation. Recruiting internally shows other employees that progression within the business is possible, which can help motivate them.

The business has to decide what form of advertising to use to publicise internal roles. There are several different options:

Key terms

Internal recruitment When a business seeks to fill a vacant position from within the business so an existing employee gains a new role within the same business — often a promotion.

External recruitment When a business recruits and employs a new person to the business who has the skills, knowledge and experience required for the job role.

NCFE Level 1/2 Technical Award in Business and Enterprise

> **Activity**
>
> Farah works for a local charity and needs to recruit a manager for a new shop that will be opening soon. The charity currently has two other shops in the city. The charity cannot afford to advertise externally and would rather recruit someone who already works for it for the role.
>
> - Advise Farah which method or methods of advertising would be suitable for this new job role for the charity. Explain your reasons.

- Notice board — Job adverts might be placed on a notice board in an area where employees will see it, for example a kitchen or staff room. Employees can then read about the job role and decide if they would like further information or want to apply.
- Newsletter — Some businesses produce a weekly, fortnightly or monthly newsletter. This gives employees information about the business and is a way of ensuring all employees receive important information. This newsletter could include a section where job adverts are placed.
- Intranet — An intranet is an internal website that can only be accessed by employees of the company. Businesses use this system to hold information and documents that employees may need for their work. An intranet may also have a section where employees can view internal job adverts. As it is an internal system, vacancies advertised in this way can only be viewed and applied for by people who have access to the intranet.
- Direct communication — A business may decide that it wants to target specific employees for job opportunities, especially if it is aware that the position may be of interest to particular individuals. In addition to wanting promotion, an employee may want to experience working in a variety of functional areas. Transferring jobs enables this to happen, as an employee can be transferred from one function to another to develop their skills and experience. An employee's position within the business might not change when they are transferred so they may have the same level of responsibility and salary, but they will have an opportunity to find out which function they prefer working in and that best suits their knowledge and skills.

External recruitment

Sometimes a business cannot recruit the right employee internally so it has to go outside of the organisation and seek an external person who has the skills, knowledge and experience for the job role. This is called external recruitment. A business could have a wider selection of people to choose from if it recruits externally and an external candidate might have fresh ideas and be really motivated to complete the job well. There are several different methods a business can use to find the correct person for the job:

- Headhunting — In certain areas of work, there are a number of people who have specialised skills who are known to each other. If an organisation needs to recruit a new employee, it might approach someone directly and inform them about a particular role and try to persuade them to apply. The person is often known to the organisation through their work, and may possibly work for a direct competitor of the business. This is known as headhunting.
- Newspapers — There are many different types of daily and weekly newspapers, often available both in printed form and online. Some are national newspapers, such as *The Times* and *The Guardian*, which contain national and international news. Other newspapers are local newspapers, which means they are produced and circulated in a local

3 Human resource requirements for business and enterprise

area and contain news relevant to that area. There are also specialist newspapers such as *The Financial Times* and the *Times Educational Supplement*, which specialise in finance and education respectively. These are aimed at people who have an interest in the subject or work in the sector. These newspapers each have a jobs section where businesses can advertise vacancies. Sometimes the jobs are classified into different areas, such as education (teacher roles), medical (nurses, doctors, dentists), retail (shop roles), etc. Readers can then view the advertisements and contact a company to find out more information about its advertised job role.

- Trade journals — Journals are often produced for specific sectors in business, such as hospitality or medicine. Trade journals contain articles and news related specifically to the sector. These journals will often advertise job roles specific to the field of work, knowing that their readers will have an interest. The job roles could be anywhere in the world and, depending on the trade, could be very specialised.
- Careers fairs — In particular sectors of business, events may be held where many similar organisations meet to advertise their job opportunities and give careers advice, in order to attract external applications. Businesses that attend will be given a space to advertise the company, which will often include displays about the business, employees who will speak to people attending the event, and tables with documents containing information about the business and the different job roles available. The organisers of the event may arrange guest speakers or celebrities to inspire the attendees. People may attend the event from all over the country, Europe or other countries if they are keen to work in the sector.
- Shop windows — Some small businesses advertise job opportunities in the windows of local shops that are clearly visible to people passing by. This method has been used for decades. These days it is less popular but it can still be effective, especially if the job is a local, part-time role.
- Recruitment agencies — These are businesses that specialise in recruitment. The agency will have the details of many people who want to work in specific job roles and sectors of business. When a business contacts the agency to inform them that a suitable role has become available, the agency will contact potential candidates directly and forward their details on to the business that is recruiting. In this way, the agency provides a service to both parties — the business and the individual. The recruitment agency makes money through an introduction fee, paid by the company that is recruiting. This recruitment method allows a business to quickly employ new staff.
- Online — Today, many jobs are advertised on the internet. These advertisements can be accessed by anyone, wherever they are based.
  - Social media — Due to the popularity of social media, businesses have found that this is a beneficial method of advertising job roles. They will appear in the user's feed and can be clicked on to find out more information.
  - Job websites — Individuals search for the job role that they are interested in, wherever in the world, and options will often appear.

Activity

Viktor runs a small TV production company that specialises in producing documentaries about natural history. He has a specialised team of film producers because of the locations they film in, as well as the time they spend abroad. He needs an additional producer and wants to recruit a new member to the team in the next two months.

- Advise Viktor on the different options that he could use to find the right employee to join the company.

NCFE Level 1/2 Technical Award in Business and Enterprise

People can then find out more information directly. Some of the results will appear through a recruitment agency. It is important for the person searching for a particular job role that they check where it is based, as sometimes places have the same name but are not in the area intended. For example, there is a place called Bristol in the UK, and also in the USA, Canada, Jamaica, Peru, Barbados and Costa Rica!

- Businesses' or enterprises' own websites — Businesses often advertise job vacancies on their own website. An individual may know which business they would like to work for and can therefore investigate job opportunities directly from the organisation's own website and usually look at the job information in detail.

- Job centres — Job centres assist those who are in receipt of benefits from the government and have been out of work for a period of time to find suitable work. They support individuals who are returning to work. Each person is allocated a work coach, who helps with the process of returning to work by assisting with where to find job adverts, how to apply and what to expect in an interview situation.

> **Test yourself**
>
> 1 Identify the two different ways a business can recruit staff.

> **Key term**
>
> **Stages of recruitment**
> The different processes that a business goes through to ensure it employs the right person for an advertised job role, such as devising a job advert, creating a job description, etc.

3.1.2 Stages of recruitment

Having the right employees working for a business is crucial for its continued success, so it is important to employ people who have the required skills and knowledge. Businesses need to attract the best people to apply for its job roles and then, after interviewing, to offer the job to the successful person. Below are the **stages of recruitment** that a business will follow. These stages can take time, but the right person must be found.

1 Identify a vacancy — The first stage is to identify that a new person is needed within the business. An organisation may have a vacancy because an employee has left the company, gained a promotion, retired or been dismissed, or a new job role may have been created because the business has expanded. For example, the popularity of the NCFE Technical Award in Business and Enterprise may mean that a new Business teacher is needed at your school.

2 Develop a person specification — A person specification is a document that identifies the skills, experience, qualifications and attributes the future employee will need in order to do the job successfully. These qualities are then split into two categories: essential, which means that the person must have these skills and experience, and desirable, meaning that it would be useful if they have the qualities. A person specification is made available to people applying for the job role (known as applicants) so that they are aware of the qualities required and can determine if they are suitable for the role.

3 Develop a job description — This document states the title of the job and describes the tasks that form the job role and the responsibilities of the employee, for example how many other employees they would be responsible for, as well as whom the successful applicant will be managed by (known as their 'direct report').

3 Human resource requirements for business and enterprise

4 Advertise the vacancy — A business needs to decide if the job is going to be advertised internally or externally (see Section 3.1.1). A job advert needs to contain information regarding the job title, brief information about the job role, location, salary range, closing date for applications and where to send application documents (usually an email address).

5 Shortlist candidates — People who apply for a job role will often be asked to send a completed application form or personal statement that outlines their skills, experience and attributes and why they would be suitable for the job role, along with their curriculum vitae (CV). A CV is a document that contains the applicant's personal details (name, address, telephone number and email address), and lists their qualifications and experience (past jobs), as well as providing references (see below). Shortlisting candidates involves the business reviewing applications against the person specification, and then deciding whom it should interview. A business will not normally be able to interview everyone who applies for a job role, especially if there are hundreds of applicants, so the best-fit ones will be shortlisted and invited to attend an interview.

6 Testing — A business may decide to ask candidates to complete a variety of assessment tasks prior to offering an interview. This often occurs for managerial positions. This will enable the business to gain further information about each candidate so that it can interview only the most suitable. The tests could be a range of individual and group activities, with candidates being observed when completing the tasks.

7 Conduct interviews — Once the business has shortlisted its chosen candidates, it invites them to come in for an interview, during which it will ask them a series of questions based on their application documents (their application form or personal statement and CV). The responses of the person being interviewed (the interviewee) will help the interviewers (the people asking the questions, who work for the business) decide if the interviewee could complete the job role. An interview will often be conducted by two or more people from the business, so that once the interviews have taken place, they can discuss who would be most suitable for the job.

8 Obtain references — When applicants apply for a job role, they give the names and contact details of two referees. A referee is a person, often a previous employer, who will provide information regarding the applicant's skills and knowledge. Referees may also need to provide more specific information about the individual relating to the job role. The business will contact the referees once other stages of the recruitment process have been completed. If the references are not very complimentary about the person, or do not match what was said in the interview, a business may decide not to offer the individual the job role.

9 Offer the position — Once the interviews and the discussion between the interviewers have taken place, and references have been obtained, the successful candidate is offered the job.

10 Issue contract — Once the successful candidate has accepted the role, the business will issue a contract to them. This is a legally binding document in which the employer and employee agree to the terms and conditions of employment. (See Section 3.1.3 for more information on contracts.)

> **Activity**
>
> Produce a poster that shows the different stages of the recruitment process, with a short explanation of each stage to show your understanding.

> **Activity**
>
> Produce a job advert and a job description for a sales assistant in a busy local takeaway. You can choose the type of food that the takeaway produces. Think about how you could attract a person to apply for the position.

79

NCFE Level 1/2 Technical Award in Business and Enterprise

Finding a suitable candidate for a job is important for a business. It could be a real problem for an organisation if the wrong person is given the job, as they may not be able to complete the job role. If the person repeatedly completes tasks incorrectly, they may have to be dismissed and the recruitment process would have to start again, which takes a lot of time as well as expense.

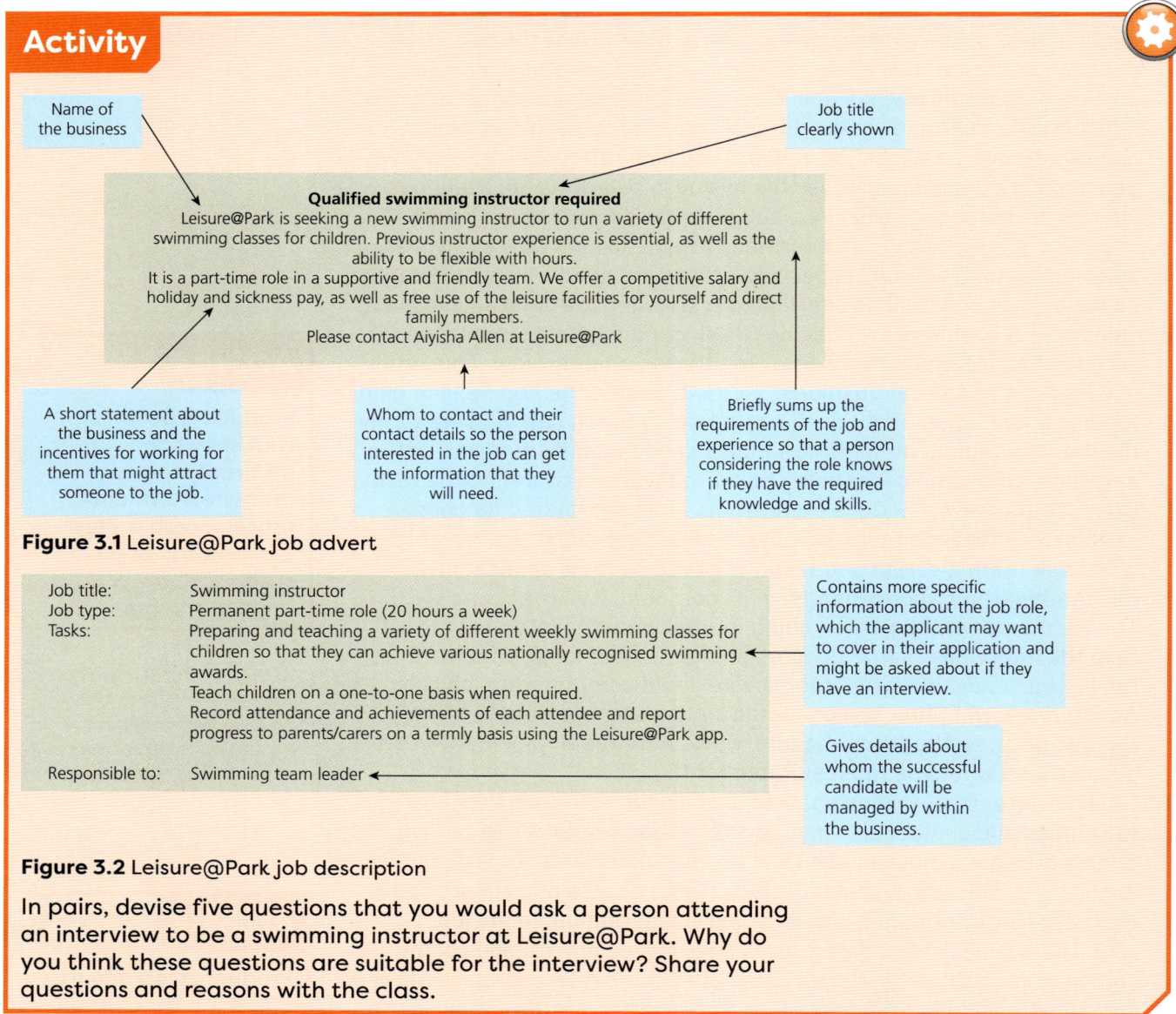

Figure 3.1 Leisure@Park job advert

Figure 3.2 Leisure@Park job description

In pairs, devise five questions that you would ask a person attending an interview to be a swimming instructor at Leisure@Park. Why do you think these questions are suitable for the interview? Share your questions and reasons with the class.

Test yourself

1. Complete the following sentence: The stage within the recruitment process that reduces the number of applicants to be interviewed is called _____.
2. Explain why it is important to obtain references prior to offering a job and issuing a contract to a successful candidate.

3.1.3 Types of employment contract

All businesses must follow the laws relating to the recruitment of staff to ensure that it is fair for all employees. Once a person is offered a job, they will agree the working arrangements with the employer and sign a **contract of employment**. It contains:

- the agreed terms and conditions of employment, including if the job is full- or part-time
- the hours that will be worked
- the location of the job
- the pay
- the holiday and sickness pay
- the holiday/bank holiday entitlement.

Once the new employee and employer have signed the document, it is legally binding.

Businesses use several types of contracts.

Key term

Contract of employment A formal document, which both the employee and employer sign, agreeing to the terms and conditions of the job.

Permanent contract

A permanent contract means the employee is employed by the business for an unlimited length of time. The contract will end when the employee leaves; for example because they have been promoted or got another job with a different company. Having a permanent contract offers the employee security in their job and stability for the business.

Temporary contract

A temporary contract is given to an employee who is required to work for the business for a certain length of time. Temporary contracts have a start and a finish date and are normally for a short period of time, such as a number of weeks or months. These contracts are often used at busy times of the year, for example in a restaurant at Christmas when it needs extra employees, or to fill gaps in staffing, such as when staff are on holiday or on maternity or parental leave.

Freelance contract

A freelance contract is when an individual works for a business for a short period of time. Such individuals are often self-employed so will pay their own income taxes. They are hired for the knowledge and services that they can provide for a specific project, for example reviewing the manuscript of a book. The freelance contract means that the individual will not be entitled to the same rights as other employees of the business, such as sick or holiday pay.

Activity

A busy greetings card-printing business requires some new employees as it is expanding. It has realised that it needs some people all year around, as well as others at specific busy times of the year. The job roles are:
- An office manager to run the busy office.
- A sales consultant responsible for gaining new customers to stock the business's greetings cards.
- A Christmas card designer in the summer months to design the new cards.
- A birthday card print operative to print the birthday cards.
- A Christmas card print operative to print the Christmas cards.

Write an email to the business manager, Brian Wilkinson, explaining the different types of contracts that would be suitable for the above jobs so that this information can be placed in the relevant recruitment documents.

Fixed-term contract

A fixed-term contract is similar to a temporary contract in that it has a pre-defined end date but is usually longer than a temporary contract. For example, a business may want to employ a person for six months as it is having a new software system installed and needs an expert to set up and maintain the system while the permanent employees are trained in its use. In this case, the business would issue a fixed-term contract to the expert. A business may also issue a fixed-term contract to cover parental leave (as an alternative to a temporary contract). Taxes will be paid by the employer and the person will receive the same benefits as the organisation's other employees, such as sick and holiday pay.

Part-time and full-time contracts

Part-time employees work only a certain number of hours per week, which will be fewer than a person who works for the business full time. Part-time work is often helpful for a business, as it allows it flexibility, and for the employee, as it means their job can fit in with their life. For example, a supermarket that is open every day may employ people to work weekends and after 6 p.m., allowing the business to remain open during these times.

Full-time employees work a number of hours determined by the business, often Monday to Friday from 9 a.m. to 5 p.m. According to the UK government website, 'a full-time worker will usually work 35 hours or more per week' (source: www.gov.uk/part-time-worker-rights).

Zero-hours contracts

Zero-hours contracts are becoming more common. This is when a business gives an individual a contract, but the hours they are required to work are not stated on the contract and are at the business's discretion. The hours can change from day to day and week to week. No maximum or minimum hours are detailed. These contracts mean that a business can offer a few days' work and the employee can either agree or disagree to the work. This gives flexibility to the employer, as it only needs to pay employees when they work and does not have to provide benefits such as holiday or sick pay. If the employee constantly refuses work, the employer may decide that it does not want to keep offering them work and can terminate the contract. The disadvantage to this sort of contract are that the individual is not guaranteed any work so there is no job security and they will not receive employee benefits such as sick pay or holiday pay.

3 Human resource requirements for business and enterprise

Activity

Office manager required at ABC Plumbing for maternity cover. £25,000 pro rata with generous holiday allowance. Please email ABCPlumbing@jobs.com

Wanted Beach hut cleaners in Devon during the busy summer months. Contact David on 08763 476525 if you are interested.

Due to an expansion in the business, T & J Co. require a production assistant to work in a busy family-run gift company. Five days a week, 9–5pm. If you are a team player, motivated to work hard and want to progress within a successful business, email T&JCo@recruitment.com for more information.

Look at the three job advertisements above and, using the information on pages 81–82, identify what contracts of employment would be suitable for each job, giving reasons for your answers.

Remember

- There are two methods of recruiting employees — internal and external recruitment.
- It is important to recruit the right employees, as it takes both time and money for the business to complete the different stages of recruitment.
- There are ten stages in the recruitment process:
  - Identifying the vacancy
  - Developing a person specification
  - Developing a job description
  - Advertising the vacancy
  - Shortlisting candidates
  - Testing
  - Interviewing
  - Obtaining references
  - Offering the position
  - Issuing a contract to the successful candidate
- There are several different types of employment contracts, which are:
  - permanent
  - temporary
  - freelance
  - fixed-term
  - full-time
  - part-time
  - zero-hours.

Test yourself

1. Define a contract of employment.
2. What is the difference between a zero-hours contract and a temporary contract?

3.2 Staff development and monitoring

3.2.1 Methods of staff development and monitoring

Staff development

It is the employer's responsibility to ensure employees keep up to date with their training, as well as to give staff the opportunity to gain further qualifications to help them complete their jobs and improve the knowledge and efficiency of the business. Staff development is good for individual employees, as it keeps them motivated and interested in their role. It is also good for the company, as these newly learnt skills and knowledge can be used within the business. In schools and colleges, teachers and lecturers go on continuing professional development (CPD) courses to learn about new qualifications or gain further understanding of the examinations and new resources to help them teacher and support their students to get the best results. Learning does not stop when you leave school! There are several forms of training.

Internal training

Internal training takes place at the business location, as the trainers are either from within the business or come into the business. For example, if a new piece of equipment is needed for use by a team of employees, the person responsible for the equipment may have the responsibility to train team members in how to use it so they all have the same knowledge and skills.

External training

External training is when employees go to a location outside of the office or business premises and receive training from external trainers. This could be a specialist course taught by experts from another business. An employee who has taken on responsibility for being a first aider for their business, for example, may have to go on a business first aid course so they know what to do if someone is injured at work. After the course, they would go back to work and use their new knowledge and skills as part of their job.

External training costs businesses in time and money, as an employee must take time away from their job to complete the course. The business may consider employing a temporary member of staff to cover the absent person or may ask other employees to take on extra tasks while they are away. The employer will also have to cover the cost of the course, as it is part of the employee's development.

> **Key terms**
>
> **Internal training** When employees receive training at the business location, from trainers who are either from within the business or who come into the business to deliver the training.
>
> **External training** When employees go to a location outside of the office or business premises and receive training from external trainers.

3 Human resource requirements for business and enterprise

Induction training

When a new member of staff starts at an organisation, they are often given **induction training** to introduce them to the different aspects of the business that they will need to know about. A typical induction might include:

- Introductions to the key members of staff that new employee will be working with, such as their managers, deputy managers and team.
- How the business is organised, the functional areas and a history of the company.
- The business policies, for example health and safety.
- The key expectations of employees and the employer.
- A tour of the business so that they know how to get around the workplace and where key people are based.
- The allocation of a mentor (if appropriate).

A business may also include specific training related to the individual's role.

The key to a successful induction is to ensure that new employees feel welcome within the organisation and have all the necessary information they need to start completing their role as soon as they can.

Key term

Induction training Training that gives new employees specific information about the business and how to complete their job role.

Staff appraisals

Each employee within a business will have a regular form of appraisal. An appraisal is a review of an employee's performance that often takes place once a year or, in some cases, twice a year. Appraisals are a formal process and the outcomes are recorded. Appraisals are completed by the employee's supervisor, so if they are based within a team it could be done by their team leader. Appraisals are a positive form of training as they give an opportunity for the employee to discuss the highlights of their performance and the areas that may need improvement.

To prepare for the appraisal, the employee may be asked to identify how they have achieved their targets and, if targets have not been met, the reasons for this. During the appraisal, the employee can refer to these prepared documents. The employee may also be asked to identify any training that they require, and why. A discussion will take place regarding their future targets, performance and training needs. This is then formally agreed and documents completed. These are reviewed at the next appraisal meeting.

Promotion

Promotion is a form of staff development. When an individual successfully applies for a more senior role, they will complete a period of training to ensure that they have the required specific skills and knowledge to successfully complete the role.

Mentoring

Mentoring is when a junior member of staff is paired with an experienced member of the team for an amount of time to learn new skills and knowledge. If any problems occur related to the job role, the employee can discuss these with their mentor. This can develop both members of staff.

NCFE Level 1/2 Technical Award in Business and Enterprise

Activity

Read the following scenarios and decide what form of training would be suitable for each individual. Justify your decision.

- Raj has recently started at the company and is unsure how to use the spreadsheet program that the business uses. He speaks to his manager, who suggests that he needs training specifically on the software.
- David is keen to go into management, but is aware that his current qualifications and experience do not reflect his potential abilities. He speaks to his manager, who says they would support any further training.
- Pilar and her sister run a small business but want to expand to remain competitive. She needs some specific business training related to expanding a small business and wants to look at different options.

Case study

As an employer of around 3000 people in the UK alone, Heinz has always made a significant investment in external training. Time pressures, however, mean that releasing staff to undertake courses is a constant challenge. At the same time, the company has been seeking ways to make the most of the wealth of knowledge, expertise and skills within its workforce.

Heinz introduced the concept of Learning Bitez, which consists of 1–4-hour workshops that are run internally by staff at the company. Topics range from IT skills and knowledge to can-making.

Staff find out about the workshops available via internal communications and then book, with the approval of their line manager, through an online system. The HR department manages the booking process.

The best measurement of short bursts of training is immediate feedback and ongoing popularity, and Pat Rees, Heinz's talent manager, says that both demonstrate staff enthusiasm for the training.

'Learning Bitez have been around for a year but they have made such an impact it is as if they've always been there,' says Rees. 'There's an agility about the way the courses start and I'd like to keep this so the training is always done by someone with a passion. Internal staff know their audiences, they already know where the problems are and how they can tailor their information.'

Val Lowe is HR administrator at Heinz. 'I did the personal effectiveness Learning Bite in November. The course leader took us through the ways in which Outlook had been dominating our days and how we could organise our time better,' she says.

'We looked at to-do lists and tasks, how to arrange diaries and get emails under control. I used to keep about 300 emails on my system and now I've got that down to about ten,' Lowe adds.

'I've also learned to turn off my email alert and to take a more disciplined approach by only looking at my emails at set times in the day. That way, I'm able to concentrate on the task I'm doing and not get distracted. I sift through and copy them into task lists.'

Source: www.hrmagazine.co.uk/article-details/learning-and-development-case-study-heinz-a-training-scheme-full-of-beans

Answer the following questions:

1. Why do you think that the Learning Bitez at Heinz have worked for:
   a. the employees
   b. the employer, Heinz?
   Explain your answers.
2. One of the factory sites in the UK started the concept of Learning Bitez at Heinz. Why do you think other sites might have been interested in using the same idea?
3. What are the advantages and disadvantages of completing internal training?
4. How do you think that your school or college could internally train its staff?

3 Human resource requirements for business and enterprise

> **Case study**
>
> Marco Perio owns and runs a barbers and hairdressing salon. He started his business in 2010 with his aim being to double his business. His success has meant that he is in a position to open another barbers and salon in a different area of the city. Marco has always ensured his employees are well trained and given them all opportunities to improve and develop their skills and knowledge within the business, which can then be used to train newer members of the teams. He ensures all employees know the basic skills required to work in both the salon and the barbers so that they can fill in if anyone is absent from work, rather than needing to use temporary members of staff. Marco needs more staff for the new premises. He hopes that some employees might want to apply for promotions in the business, but he recognises that new members of staff will also be required.
> He needs the following employees:
> - A salon and barber manager
> - Three salon stylists
> - A senior barber
> - Two barbers
> - Two hairdressing assistants to wash hair, clean up, etc.
>
> Answer the following questions:
> 1. Explain to Marco the differences between internal and external recruitment methods.
> 2. Advise Marco what his options are for finding the right staff to complete the different roles. What would you suggest for the different roles?
> 3. New staff will need to have an induction training programme. You have been given responsibility for compiling the induction day for the new salon. What will the new employees need to know in order to complete their jobs? Devise the induction day, thinking about the different themes and the timings. Produce a document that clearly shows the plan for the day that will ensure Marco's new staff will be inducted efficiently so they can start working as soon as possible.
> 4. As the business has expanded, Marco knows that he must start to make certain processes more formal. He wants to introduce an appraisal system into the business, but he does not know what this entails. Write an email to him explaining what appraisal is and the benefits to his employees of this system.

Monitoring of staff

Disciplinary action

It is important for a business to monitor its staff to ensure that they are performing well for the business. If employers are not happy with the performance of individuals or a team, they may decide to implement disciplinary action. The series of steps that the business will go through to try and resolve the issues is shown in Figure 3.3.

For example, if an employee constantly arrives late to work, a business will want to discuss this with them and may issue a formal warning, meaning that if they do not improve their punctuality, further action will be taken against them, which could ultimately result in them losing their job.

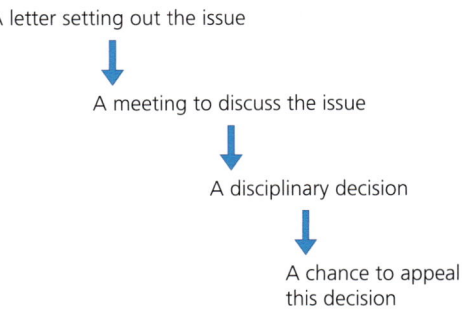

Figure 3.3 Steps in disciplinary action (Source: www.gov.uk/disciplinary-procedures-and-action-at-work/how-disciplinary-procedures-work)

Dismissal

Dismissal is when an individual loses their job because the business no longer wants to employ them. The Human Resources functional area is responsible for dismissing employees. For example, if an employee continued to break the business's rules or conditions that they agreed when they joined the business, they could be dismissed.

Test yourself

1. Write a definition of internal training.
2. Write a definition of external training.
3. Why is induction training important for a new employee?
4. Identify the type of staff development from the following description: A junior member of staff has been paired with an experienced member of the team for an amount of time to learn new skills and knowledge.
5. What are the different stages of disciplinary action?

Remember

- There are two forms of training: internal or external to the business.
- Induction training occurs when an employee first starts at a business.
- Staff appraisals are a positive method of staff development.
- Promotion is a form of staff development as an employee will move to a more senior position and receive a period of training to ensure that the individual has the skills and knowledge to successfully complete the role.
- Mentoring is when a junior member of staff is paired with an experienced member of the team for an amount of time to learn new skills and knowledge.
- There are four stages within a disciplinary procedure:
  - A letter is sent setting out the issue.
  - A meeting occurs to discuss the issue.
  - A disciplinary decision is made.
  - Finally, there is a chance to appeal the decision.
- Dismissal is when an individual loses their job because the business no longer wants to employ them.

3.3 Motivation

3.3.1 Financial methods of motivation

Employees work for a business in order to earn money that they can then use to live on. The job role determines the amount of money that the employee earns. The way in which a business pays its staff depends on the individual business.

Wages

An employee who earns a wage will often be paid on a weekly basis. The rate that is paid per hour is multiplied by the number of hours that were worked that week. All businesses have to pay the minimum wage. This means that no business is legally allowed to pay its employees less than the amount stated by the government. (For more on the minimum wage, see Section 7.1.1.)

Salaries

Salaries are paid monthly. The amount that an employee is paid per year is displayed as an annual salary. This is divided into twelve equal payments and generally the employee is paid the same amount each month, on the same date and in the same way. If the employee takes an agreed holiday, this does not affect the amount that they are paid that month, as paid holiday is part of their contract. Knowing how much they will be paid each month can help people to budget and save.

Piece rate

Piece rate pay is when an employee is paid for the quantity of units (products) that they complete. This method of pay means that the employee gets paid for the amount of work that they produce, which could encourage some employees to work quickly to get paid more. However, they may not produce good quality units if they have rushed their work to complete more units. If the goods do not meet the required standard, this could affect the business as customers will not be happy and not want to purchase products from it again, which could affect its profits.

Hourly rate

A business may pay an individual a set hourly rate. This means that if they had a contract where they had to work 20 hours a week, the business would pay them a specific hourly rate for those set hours that they worked.

Performance-related pay

Performance-related pay is when an employee is rewarded for their individual performance at work. It could be that an employee exceeds the employer's expectations and receives a monetary reward. For example, a voucher for a product that they can choose up to a certain amount. This system of pay has to be regularly monitored by management to ensure it is fair for all the employees who are paid using this method. There is a danger that this system encourages working in a more individual way, rather than working together as a team.

Bonuses

A bonus is an amount of money that is added to a person's normal pay as a reward for good work. A company might choose to pay this at a certain time each year or if it has done particularly well. If the business is running at a loss and cannot afford it, it would not be a good idea to give a bonus, no matter how hard the employees are working! A bonus motivates staff to keep working hard for the business and may maintain their loyalty, knowing that more bonuses could be given in the future.

Commission

In some areas of business, often in sales roles, employees are paid a basic salary and, for every sale they make, a certain percentage of the sale is also given to the employee. This is called a commission. It encourages employees to work hard because the more sales they make, the more commission they will receive. However, sometimes this form of pay encourages aggressive selling, meaning that customers are put under pressure to buy something that maybe they do not want or need.

NCFE Level 1/2 Technical Award in Business and Enterprise

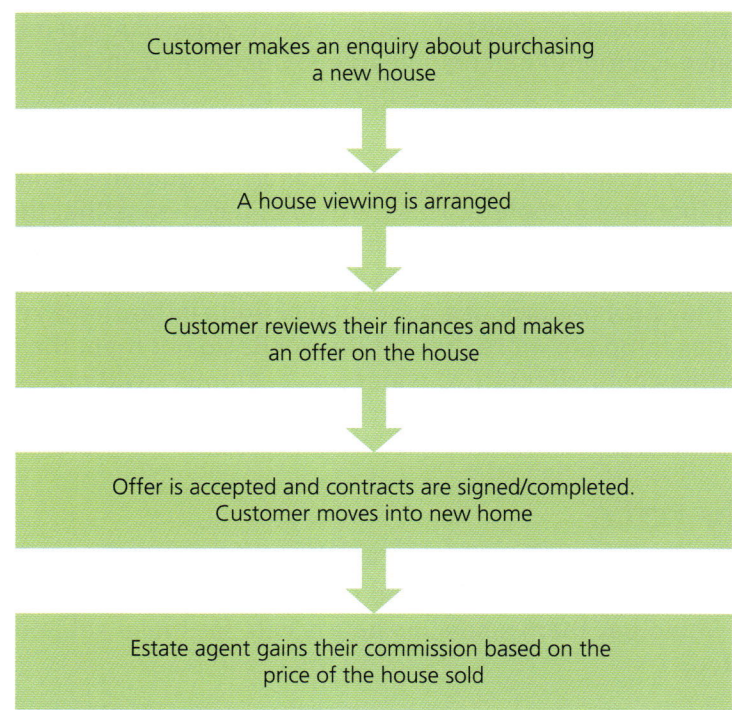

Figure 3.4 An example of business commissions

Test yourself

1. What are the main differences between a wage and a salary?

Profit sharing

Profit sharing is when all employees receive an amount of the business's profits each year, meaning that the profits are shared. The amount of profit received will be determined by the employee's job role, so a manager may receive more of the profits than a junior member of staff. If the company makes a loss, there will be no profits to share. This form of pay can therefore be a motivator for the business.

Activity

Looking back at the definitions of the financial methods, identify which form is relevant to each of the following people:

a Aine works in a car showroom selling expensive cars. Each month her sales targets are reviewed and she is rewarded if she has exceeded her targets.

b Tricia is the manufacturing manager in a large company and has to work long hours. She enjoys working for the business and has been there for five years.

c Rikke works at her family's business. For the past few years the business has expanded and made some profits. As the business has remained profitable, it was decided at a family meeting to change the way the profits were used. Each family member now receives part of the profits, which they consider fairer as they all work very hard as a team.

d Jasper delivers leaflets to 300 houses most weeks. The number of leaflets he has to deliver differs depending on the time of year. For example, near Christmas there are more.

e Malia makes clocks for a local business out of recycled materials. She is paid for the number of clocks that she makes each day.

f Anna sells office space to new businesses. When a business signs a contract, Anna receives an amount of money for her success.

g Debbie has worked for a hat-making business for one year. She was surprised when her manager told her that she would receive some extra money for her efforts. Her manager was really pleased with the work that she had completed since arriving at the business and the new clients that it gained as a result.

3.3.2 Non-financial methods of motivation

In addition to financial incentives to motivate staff working for a business, there are also non-financial means of rewarding employees to ensure they remain motivated to work well for the success of the business.

Job rotation

Job rotation is where an employee moves to different job roles and so gains skills in different areas within the business. A company could set up a scheme where employees work in different areas for a short period of time (two or three months) to gain new knowledge and skills. This is often offered to employees who get promoted quite quickly to managerial positions, as it allows them to learn how all areas of the business operate. It could also be offered to enable an employee to determine where in a business they want to work.

Job enlargement

Job enlargement is when a specific role increases in size over time. The individual appointed to the role may have to take on more responsibility as the business grows and their team increases. This means that the individual will have to participate in a wider range of so the role will be more varied, which will hopefully motivate the employee.

Job enrichment

Job enrichment enables a business to give specific employees more tasks to complete and more responsibility. It will often occur to give the individual more of a challenge due to finding their current role restricting or repetitive. It will give the employee more motivation to continue to work hard for the business and allow them to gain new skills/knowledge.

Training

Training is when the employer pays for their staff to learn new knowledge and skills that will benefit the business. It is a motivating factor as employees will gain new skills and knowledge, and possibly qualifications, which could be used to earn promotions internally within the business or externally. Training opportunities keep employees motivated and interested in their role.

Team-working

Team-working is when individuals come together as a group to complete a range of different activities, for example a specific project. Team-working means that a range of different skills and knowledge will be present within the team as everyone has different skills. It can be a motivational method since working as a team means that the responsibility can be shared within the team and individuals can work to their strengths. Hopefully the individuals within the team will work well together to complete the project.

Empowerment

Empowerment is concerned with ensuring that an employee feels valued for the work that they have completed for a business. It can come in many forms, including:

- being effective in their role
- being in control
- influencing the success of the business.

This can be very motivational for individuals as they will feel in control of their work and valued for their efforts.

> **Test yourself**
> 1. What are the main differences between job enlargement and job enrichment?
> 2. How can team-working help in a business?

3.3.3 Motivation theories

Motivation is important in business, and as such theorists have investigated the satisfaction and motivation of employees. The two theorists that we will look at are Maslow and Herzberg.

Maslow's hierarchy of needs

Abraham Maslow (1908–70) put forward a theory that most of our actions are governed by our needs. He argued that we are motivated to satisfy a hierarchy of five sets of needs, shown in Figure 3.5.

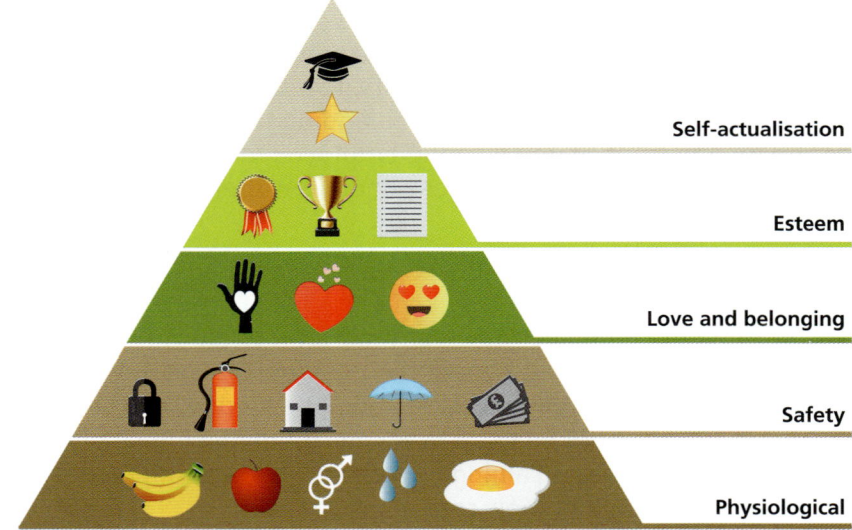

Figure 3.5 Maslow's hierarchy of needs

Maslow's hierarchy of human needs begins with the physical needs, through the social needs, towards the psychological needs. Maslow believed that each need has to be totally fulfilled before the next level of needs becomes important. By the time all the needs have fulfilled, the individual will be motivated by self-actualisation, in other words psychological growth and development. If a lower-level need becomes unfulfilled, for example there is the threat of redundancy, an individual's focus will return to basic needs, such as security.

Maslow's theory has great appeal for business. Managers can find out which level their employees are at and use this to decide on suitable rewards. There are problems, however, when Maslow's theory is used in practice. One level may be more important than another for some individuals, while some rewards fit into more than one category. For example, money can be used to fulfil basic needs but is also seen as a status symbol.

Herzberg's two-factor theory

In 1966, Frederick Herzberg (1923–2000) attempted to find out what motivated people at work. He questioned 200 accountants and engineers about the incidents in their jobs that gave them strong feelings of satisfaction or dissatisfaction. There are two parts to the theory, which are:

- motivating factors
- hygiene factors.

Motivating factors, such as recognition and added responsibility, lead to job satisfaction. Hygiene factors, such as a clean office or a pay rise, keep employees in their jobs and prevent them from becoming dissatisfied in their roles but do not motivate them to work harder.

Remember

- There are several methods of pay and remuneration, including wages, salaries, piece rates and commissions.
- Bonuses, performance-related pay and profit sharing can motivate employees to work harder for the business.
- Non-financial methods of motivation do not cost the business and can help to create a good working environment for employees.
- Maslow put forward a theory that most of our actions are governed by our needs. He argued that we are motivated to satisfy five sets of needs.
- Herzberg found that motivating factors can lead to job satisfaction, but according to his theory employees will not be motivated by hygiene factors.

Read about it

www.tutor2u.net/business/reference/people-management-methods-of-recruitment-gcse — Guidance on the different methods of recruitment.

www.bbc.com/bitesize/guides/zfhn34j/revision/2 — Tips on how staff are protected in the workplace, including employment rights and redundancy.

www.bbc.com/bitesize/guides/zn6hyrd/revision/1 — Tips on staff recruitment.

www.tutor2u.net/business/topics/remuneration — Links to a number of articles related to remuneration (money paid for work).

NCFE Level 1/2 Technical Award in Business and Enterprise

Test yourself

1. Copy the diagram below and fill in the blanks in the stages of recruitment: Testing, Obtain references, Issue contract, Identify a vacancy.

[ ] → Develop a person specification → Develop a job description → Advertise the vacancy

[ ] ← Conduct interviews ← [ ] ← Shortlist candidates

Offer the position → [ ]

2. Fill in the gaps in Maslow's hierarchy of needs.

[ ]
[ ]
Love and belonging
[ ]
[ ]

Practice questions

1. Select which **one** of the following is an internal method of recruitment. [1 mark]
   a. Headhunting
   b. Intranet
   c. Newspapers
   d. Careers fair

2. Explain **three** different forms of online recruitment. [6 marks]

3. Explain each of the following types of employment contract:
   – Permanent
   – Full-time
   – Zero-hours [6 marks]

3 Human resource requirements for business and enterprise

4 Select which **one** of the following is a method of paying an employee for the quantity of units (products) that they complete. [1 mark]
   a Wages
   b Hourly rate
   c Bonuses
   d Piece rate

5 Select which **one** of the following is a non-financial method of motivation. [1 mark]
   a Profit sharing
   b Empowerment
   c Commissions
   d Competition

6 Select how many factors there are in Herzberg's theory of motivation. [1 mark]
   a One
   b Two
   c Three
   d Four

7 Explain the financial motivational method term 'bonus' and why these are used. [3 marks]

8 Using Herzberg's motivational theory, state **one** method that a business could follow to try to improve motivation. [2 marks]

Assignment practice

Your sandwich and panini delivery business has been launched and has proved very popular. So, after a year of trading, you have decided to expand. Customers order their lunches via an app and payment is taken at the time of the order. You use a delivery van, which is small and uniquely decorated. To expand, you will need to employ more staff so that an efficient service can continue.

Tasks:

1 Describe the stages of recruitment as well as the different types of employment contract that you may decide to use for the new employees. (AO1, AO2)

2 You have successfully appointed two new staff: Michael who will work school hours and Debbie who will be full time. You need to make sure that they complete training. Create a two-day training programme for each new employee. (AO1, AO2)

3 Now that you have employees, it is important that you keep them motivated. Research different forms of motivational techniques that you could realistically introduce. Create a document that explains three different methods. (AO1, AO2, AO4)

4 Operations management

About this content area

This content area focuses on the various factors that influence the operations management decisions a business makes. You will learn about:

- Outsourcing tasks to another business — The four main reasons for a business to outsource work: quality, cost, speed and flexibility.
- The various lean production methods — The different methods of lean production: just-in-time production, cell production and kaizen.
- Maintaining and improving quality — The difference between quality control and quality assurance.
- Production methods — The different ways that a business can produce products, including job, batch, flow production and mass customisation.
- Customer service — The importance of good customer service and how this is measured by a business to benefit both it and its customers.

4.1 Operations management

4.1.1 Outsourcing

When organisations grow, they may not be able to complete all of the business tasks themselves. One way to cover these tasks is to outsource some operations. This means the organisation hires another business to do some of the work for it, for example payroll operations, IT operations or website design. This is because these operations require specialised knowledge and experience that take years of training. Small businesses, for example sole traders such as plumbers, builders and electricians, also outsource various aspects of their work as they do not have all of the necessary skills to do this work themselves. The outsourced work is usually of high quality but is considerably more expensive than if it was completed in-house.

There are four main reasons for a business to outsource work, which are detailed below.

Quality

It is important for a business to ensure that the products/services associated with it are of high quality. This is because any quality issues can affect the perception of the business for future sales. Quality assurance is complex and time consuming, so a business may decide to outsource quality control to another specialist business. This allows the employees within the business to focus on their normal tasks.

Cost

If a business is considering outsourcing one element, the financial implications of doing so will be a major consideration. The cost of outsourcing may be a one-off cost or an ongoing cost that the business pays each month, depending on the services that it requires and the frequency of the service.

For example, if a business wants to complete some comprehensive primary market research about a new product, it may decide to outsource this to a company that specialises in completing primary research. This would be a one-time event.

Alternatively, a business may decide to outsource the monthly pay process, known as payroll, to another business as it may not have the expertise within the company. This will ensure that all employees get paid the right amount for the role that they complete. This will be an ongoing cost to the business.

Speed

Outsourcing can speed up the process of business. If employees are not involved in the production of one aspect of the business because it has been outsourced, they can concentrate on other areas of the business.

For example, if a business produces hampers for different occasions, it may use another business to create the baskets as it does not have the expertise to make them itself or because it does not have facilities to make as many baskets as it needs. The business would be reliant on the outsourced business to produce and deliver the baskets on time to ensure that they can be filled with the required products and sent to customers to fulfil orders. Enlisting the services of another business will speed up the production of products for customers.

Flexibility

Outsourcing means that a business can use the services of other businesses for the time that it requires them and, if necessary, can change supplier. It may, for example, change supplier if there is an increase in the cost of the outsourced services. The business could also decide to train employees to complete these outsourced activities instead. This is the choice of the business as it has this flexibility. It will need to check the terms and conditions of the contract with the outsourced business.

Activity

Caroline runs an animal sanctuary. It is a busy business and recently she has seen an increase in the range of different animals that she and the staff she employs have to care for. Staff are currently completing a range of different qualifications to enhance their skills and knowledge to cope with the demands of the business. This means that they cannot complete some of the routine tasks they normally complete, which include cleaning the animal areas and feeding and ordering the range of food required for the different animals.

- Caroline is wondering what to do. Write an email to Caroline explaining how outsourcing some of the activities could help the animal sanctuary.

4.1.2 Lean production

Lean production is a management approach that aims to cut waste and focus on high quality. The idea is used throughout a business, from design to distribution. There are different methods of lean production, including just-in-time (JIT) production, cell production and kaizen.

JIT production

Just-in-time (JIT) production means that stock or materials arrives on the production line just as it is needed. This minimises the amount of stock and materials that have to be stored, and so reduces storage costs such as a warehouse. JIT has many benefits and may appear an obvious way to organise production, but it is a complicated process that requires efficient handling. It is important that a business can meet the required demand from its customers and manage the cash flow within the business.

Table 4.1 Advantages and disadvantages of JIT production

Advantages	Disadvantages
Improves cash flow as stock is not tied up in storage	Needs suppliers and stock-ordering systems to be reliable
Reduces waste — stock does not go out of date	May be difficult to manage if there are surges in demand
Requires less factory storage space	Potential for loss of reputation if orders are delivered late

Cell production

Cell production is the opposite of production-line production process and works as follows:

- The production process is divided into a series of stages.
- Production is arranged around teams.
- Each team completes a full unit of production, instead of individuals completing one task.
- Each team has responsibility for their work and can see end results.
- It increases motivation as the workers are skilled in all areas.
- It is flexible, as if one person is away then another member can fill in as they are all trained in the different parts.
- It increases responsibility as there are different skills required for the different parts.
- It improves quality.

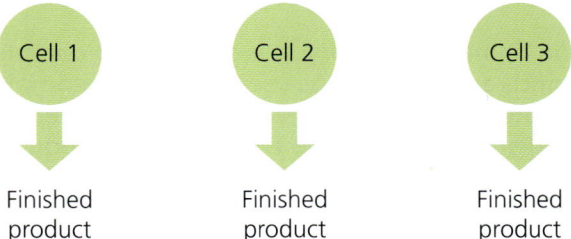

Figure 4.1 Cell production

For example, a piano business is able to assemble six pianos using six different cells. Each cell takes all the separate elements, with all members of the cell being trained on all the steps. Once the whole process has been completed, six pianos have been made.

Kaizen

Kaizen is a Japanese concept that focuses on gradual and continuous improvement. The idea is a whole-business philosophy, and to ensure its success it is important that everyone in the organisation buys into the concept and vision. Using the kaizen concept a business can focus on different key areas, including reduction in waste (waste consideration), punctuality (efficiency) and future thinking (continuous development). These are important areas as they will impact on the business operations as well as enable the business to be more considerate of these three key areas.

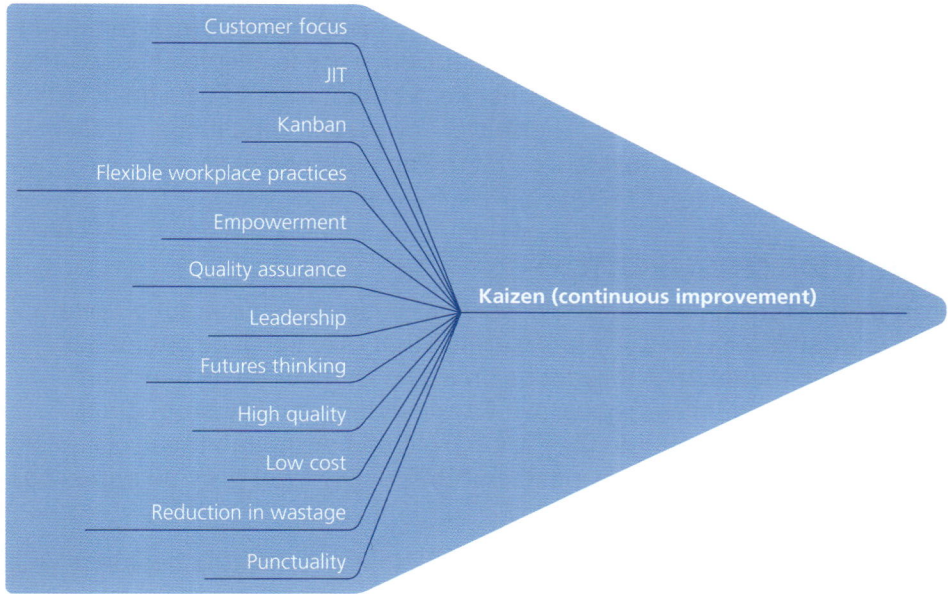

Figure 4.2 Kaizen concept

4.1.3 Maintaining and improving quality

Quality control

Quality control is an important aspect of any business. This is when an organisation checks that its products and services meet the required standards, so that customers will be satisfied when they purchase the product/service. For example, imagine if you purchased your favourite soft drink and it did not taste the same as it normally does — you may be confused. This situation would demonstrate that the quality control processes at the manufacturer were not correct. It is important, therefore, that a business ensures its quality standards are high.

How can a business check its quality standards?

A business can complete an inspection process to ensure that the quality control standards meet its requirements. For a product the inspection will focus on the goods that are produced in the manufacturing process, and as part of the inspection samples will be tested and the findings reported. This is known as sampling. For a service, a quality control check could be asking users to complete a customer satisfaction survey. If necessary, adjustments may need to be made to the current processes.

Costs

Any new process will have a financial implication in terms of cost to the business. The costs will include staff training, the possible purchase of new equipment and machinery, and the time it takes for the new processes to be up and running. If alterations are needed to the process, such as new machinery, this will be a cost to the business. However, if there are known errors in the manufacturing process and no changes are made, then the damage to the business's reputation could be significant and could affect future sales. Therefore, any recommendations made should be implemented to ensure that the quality control process is robust.

Quality assurance

Most businesses have a quality assurance system to maintain a certain level of quality for every product/service that they produce and sell. Usually, this means that they focus on every stage of the production and delivery processes. This provides consistent-quality products to their customers every time they are purchased. Although the process of quality control costs the business, but these costs will provide numerous benefits, including:

- Zero waste — If below-standard products are made, the business will need to dispose of them, which will increase the waste the business produces. This is a cost to the business, so producing less waste will be a benefit.
- Zero defects — If products are produced with faults or defects, there can be repercussions for the business in terms of its reputation, which can affect future sales. If defects are reported on a wide scale, for example if there are reports in the media about a defective product, this can have a real impact on a business as the trust will be broken between the business and its customers. This can be hard to regain.
- Right first time — A business should aim to produce products and services that are right first time, meaning that everything is perfect. It is hard for a business to maintain this but, with the right investment, the right process and the right staff involved, a business can aim to achieve this.

4.1.4 Production methods

Businesses tend to use one of the following production methods.

- Job production — This is when one product is made at a time. Every product will be slightly different and usually made by hand and/or machine. The products will be expensive and very time consuming to make. Examples of job production are pet portraits, handmade jumpers and bespoke jewellery.
- Batch production — Small quantities of identical products are made. This method uses machinery and manpower. The products tend to be relatively expensive due to the labour costs. Each batch will be slightly different. Examples of batch production are handmade chocolates, coloured paint and knitting wool.
- Flow production — This is similar to mass production, which is when large amounts of products are produced at once, except that in flow production the production line is operated 24 hours a day, 7 days a week. This reduces the costs of stopping and starting production. Very few workers are required and the majority of the work is completed by machine. Examples of flow production include canned baked beans and mass-produced loaves of bread.
- Mass customisation — This is usually completed on a production line and involves the assembly of different components or items. It is usually completed by machine and is relatively cheap to operate. Examples of mass customisation are cars, T-shirts and motorised parts.

A business will need to consider which method of production will be suitable for its enterprise activities. The business will have to consider:

- start-up costs (see Section 6.2.2 for more on costs)
- unit costs
- level of demand for the business's products
- flexibility
- time
- volume of output.

Activity

Working in pairs, write a list of businesses in your local area. Decide which of the four different production methods is used by each of the businesses you identified.

4.1.5 Customer service

Customer service is the way in which a business looks after its customers. Excellent customer service ensures that a business attracts new customers and retains its existing ones.

Giving excellent customer service will:

- promote word-of-mouth promotion
- improve the business's reputation
- encourage repeat business
- set the business apart from its competitors
- provide brand awareness
- ensure customer loyalty and encourage customers to purchase from the business in the future.

In order to provide excellent customer service, employees will need:

- good communication skills for interacting with customers
- patience to understand customers' needs and wants
- attention to detail — it is important that employees focus on customer requirements
- good product knowledge
- excellent personal presentation skills — employees need to be appropriately dressed and act in a manner that will attract and retain customers.

Many businesses treat their staff as their most valuable asset. Employees who have excellent product knowledge and who are able to engage with customers about the products and services are likely to attract and retain customers.

Businesses have learnt that it is not only important for their staff to engage with customers before and during a sale, they also need to offer excellent after-sales services too.

Businesses look to employ customer service assistants who are able to deal with exchanges and queries about deliveries and damaged products, or simply advise customers on how to use a product. These employees need to enjoy dealing with customers and be happy, friendly and helpful.

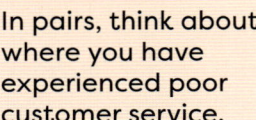

Activity

In pairs, think about where you have experienced poor customer service.

- What made it bad, and how did it make you feel about that particular business?
- What would you expect to see from excellent customer service?

Case study

The cruise industry has grown in popularity. There is now a large number of franchised cruise specialists offering cruise holidays to passengers.

In order to differentiate themselves from other travel agents, these cruise specialists offer excellent customer service. They are usually experienced cruise passengers themselves, so they can offer excellent product knowledge and are frequently available seven days a week to offer advice to passengers before they travel, during the cruise and on their return.

Answer the following question:

1. Identify and explain **three** factors that travel agents need to consider when using customer service to attract and retain customers.

A business will use a variety of different methods to monitor and measure its customer service on a regular basis. These methods include:

- Customer satisfaction scores — A business needs to consider how it will receive feedback from its customers. In recent years, many organisations have become inventive in getting customer feedback to try and make it as easy as possible for customers to engage in feedback. For example, IKEA enables shoppers to rate their shopping experience as they leave the store by pressing some emojis on a screen. This gives instant feedback to the store. Some businesses send online surveys to their customers to review their experience. Hotels are keen to do this and send guests forms to review their stay after leaving. Often there will be some type of incentive offered, such as the opportunity to win a prize or 10% off the customer's next meal.

4 Operations management

- Repeat business data — Businesses measure the number of customers who return to purchase further goods and services.
- Mystery shoppers — Individuals enter a business to make a purchase and then review the performance of the organisation in terms of how they were treated and served. The findings are then reported to the business.
- Levels of complaints/compliments — These can be gathered over a period of time and then the outcomes reviewed and reported.
- Customer surveys — These are important to businesses. Without a clear understanding of what customers need and want, a new business is unlikely to succeed. For example, an entrepreneur who opens a new children's indoor play area would be likely to conduct customer surveys to gain an understanding of customers' thoughts. They could ask a range of questions about the facilities, pricing, location and also what improvements/suggestions could be made to help the business be successful and grow in the future.

Activity

In small groups, discuss how a hotel may get feedback from its guests about the services it offers.

Remember

- Outsourcing can improve the quality, speed and flexibility of the business, but will come at a cost to the business.
- Lean production methods include JIT production, cell production and kaizen.
- Maintaining and improving quality includes quality control and quality assurance. Both will have an impact on the business's operations, hopefully in a positive way.
- A business can produce products in a range of different ways, including job, batch and flow production as well as mass customisation. The type of production method used will depend on the products and services that the business produces.
- Customer service is the way in which a business looks after its customers.
- Excellent customer service ensures that a business attracts new customers and retains its existing ones.
- In order to provide excellent customer service, employees need certain attributes, for example good communication skills, patience and attention to detail.
- Customer feedback is very important to new businesses. Without having a clear understanding of what its customers need and want, and their reactions to its products/services a new organisation is unlikely to succeed.
- Businesses have to decide how to measure quality of customer service.

Test yourself

1. What does JIT stand for?
2. What does the kaizen theory focus on?
3. How can a business maintain and improve quality?
4. Identify two different production methods used in business.
5. Write a definition of customer service.
6. List five ways that a business can deliver excellent customer service.
7. Explain three ways that employees can provide excellent customer service to their customers.
8. How can mystery shoppers help a business in terms of customer service?
9. Why are customer surveys helpful to a business?

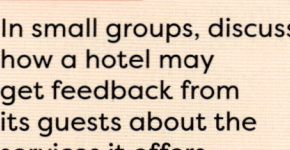

NCFE Level 1/2 Technical Award in Business and Enterprise

Read about it

Barrat, C. and Whitehead, M. *Buying for Business: Insights in purchasing and supply management* (Wiley, 2004) — Answers to key questions about purchasing and supply management in organisations.

Emmett, S. *Supply Chain in Ninety Minutes* (Management Books, 2004) — A concise practical introduction to supply chain management.

Green, J. *Starting Your Own Business* (How to Books, 2011) — A step-by-step guide to how an entrepreneur should set up a business.

Heppell, M. *Five Star Service: How to deliver exceptional customer service* (Pearson Business, 2015) — How businesses can ensure they deliver excellent customer service.

Hughes, V. and Weller, D. *Set Up a Successful Small Business* (Teach Yourself, 2010) — Guidance and advice on how an entrepreneur should set up a small business.

www.gov.uk/browse/business — Useful information about different business operations.

www.socialenterprise.org.uk — Excellent practical examples from a national body for social enterprise.

www.salesforce.com/products/service-cloud/best-practices/important-customer-service-skills-list — Explains the importance of customer service skills.

Practice questions

1. Identify **three** lean production methods. [3 marks]
2. State **three** features of cell production. [3 marks]
3. What is the difference between quality control and quality assurance? [4 marks]
4. Identify and explain **three** different types of production method. [6 marks]

Assignment practice

Your sandwich and panini delivery business has been launched and has proved very popular and after a year of trading you have decided to expand. Customers order their lunches via an app and payment is taken at the time of the order. You have expanded by employing two new staff. You recognise that the operation of the business is very important for the business to continue to grow.

Tasks:

1. Businesses use different forms of production. Research which forms of production may or may not be appropriate for your business. (AO1, AO2)
2. Recently you have asked for feedback via the ordering app on the customer service that customers have received. The results have been mixed. Research some businesses that have received excellent customer service ratings and consider how your business could achieve this for every order it receives. (AO1, AO2)

3. You need to monitor customer service. Investigate the different methods that you could use and decide which method you think will be best, justifying your decision. (AO1, AO2, AO3)

5 Business growth

> **About this content area**
>
> This content area focuses on the business and enterprise growth that an enterprise will need to understand if it wants to continue to grow in the future. You will learn about:
>
> - Internal and external growth — The differences between internal and external growth and the various ways in which these can occur.
> - Economies and diseconomies of scale — How economies and diseconomies of scale can affect a business and their impacts.
> - The challenges of growth — The challenges that must be considered whenever a business grows and the costs to a business of expansion.

5.1 Business and enterprise growth

Once a new business is established, it may wish to grow. Growth can be internal or external. Both are important for a business if it wants to continue to succeed and develop.

5.1.1 Internal growth

Internal growth occurs when a business expands (increases number of customers, revenue, profits) through increasing its own activities, as opposed to merging or taking over another company (i.e. external growth). Internal growth can be measured in four areas.

> **Key term**
>
> **Internal growth** How a business has grown from where it originally started to the current time and where it strives to be in the future.

Developing new products

A business may have a very successful brand and decide to create new products within the same brand portfolio to develop the business. Apple is famous for producing computers, and smartphones, but it also makes other products and accessories such as Airpods.

Updating current products

A business might have a food product that sells very well and decide to change an ingredient to make a new product. With consumer awareness now meaning businesses are focusing on the amount of sugar in products, an organisation may reduce the sugar content of its products, which could result in a brand new product being produced alongside the original product. For example, Heinz now produce a 50 per cent less salt and sugar tomato ketchup which sells alongside the original sauce.

Entering new markets

A business that wants to continue to develop and grow will need to review the products and services that it currently provides and decide how it may be able to develop these for different markets. This could involve focusing on a different age group or gender or considering expansion into international markets.

For example, a cheese-making business that supplies local delicatessens and restaurants may decide to offer a cheese subscription service to customers within the UK, who can then sample a range of chesses on a three- or four-monthly basis. This would be an example of a business identifying and entering a new target market.

Geographical expansion

When a business first starts, it could be run from a small office in a shared building or even from a garden shed. If the business is successful, however, such a location may become too small and additional space may be required in another location. A business may need to find premises to store stock of its products. It may then continue to expand and open more outlets around the UK and maybe eventually internationally. This is known as geographical expansion.

For example, a form of geographical expansion would be if a café opened on a local high street. After a year it becomes so successful that it opens another branch in a different area of the town, and six months later expands its business into the next town.

5.1.2 External growth

External growth is when a business grows by buying or taking over other organisations, enabling it to expand its operations quickly. External growth can increase a business's sales and subsequent profit, making it more dominant in the markets it operates in.

Mergers

Mergers are a form of external growth where two businesses voluntarily decide to become one organisation. This may mean that the new, merged business becomes stronger as it combines what the two businesses own, the expertise of both companies' staff, and the opportunities of new products and services. This is not guaranteed, though, and it could mean that:

- job losses occur because staff in both companies hold the same jobs
- disagreements occur due to the different ways in which the companies were run
- share prices reduce because investors may worry about the merger and want to pull out of the business.

Activity

Research four different businesses that have either:
- developed a new product
- updated their current products
- entered a new market
- expanded geographically.

Make notes on each business and be prepared to share your thoughts with the rest of the class.

Test yourself

1. Write a definition of internal growth.
2. Explain why a business may decide to develop a new product.
3. Explain an example of a business expanding geographically.

Key terms

External growth Business growth by buying or taking over other businesses.

Merger A form of external growth for two businesses that voluntarily decide to become one organisation.

An example of a successful merger is that of Disney and Pixar. They merged in 2006 and since then have produced many successful children's films. Both were successful in their own right, but the merger allowed them to combine the expertise of their employees to dominate a competitive market.

Takeovers

A **takeover** is when a successful business acquires control of another business due to the circumstances it finds itself in. This became more common during the Covid-19 pandemic as businesses struggled to survive due to worldwide lockdowns. One reason why companies may be taken over is because they have become vulnerable due to changes in the way consumers shop. As more consumers chose to shop online, some high street shops saw their sales and profits falling. This impacted on these businesses as some companies just did not seem as relevant and their products/services did not appeal to customers.

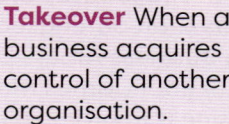

Key term

Takeover When a business acquires control of another organisation.

Businesses that remain relevant and able to compete against online markets can potentially acquire control of organisations that are struggling. This can enable the successful business to grow and develop into new markets, increasing its market share and bringing different brands to its consumers. It will cost the business, however, as some employees might disagree with the takeover and leave, or roles may be duplicated in the business that has been taken over. Alternatively, employees could see a takeover as an opportunity for them personally as well as for the business.

Examples of recent takeovers include:

- Sainsbury's bought Argos and Habitat for £1.4 billion in September 2016.
- The Co-op bought Nisa Local for £143 million in 2017.
- Hilco, an Australian company, bought Homebase for £1 in May 2018.
- ASOS bought Topshop and other brands from Arcadia for £330 million in February 2021.

Joint ventures

Joint ventures are when two businesses join together to complete a project. The businesses remain independent of each other. The project could be a long-term or short-term project. For example, a company might want to complete some research with a similar company, which then can share the findings and use them to benefit its own business. Companies might do this to save money, as completing something jointly means the costs are shared. Google and NASA, for example, formed a joint venture when they created Google Earth in the mid-2000s. This is still a popular resource and is used by millions of people each year.

Case study

SpudULike was a successful fast-food business that started in 1974 selling jacket potatoes with different fillings to its customers. It had branches all over the UK, but as other fast-food businesses became popular the humble baked potato did not seem as appealing to customers. Branches started to close and, in 2019, the business went into administration.

However, the journey did not end for SpudULike, as it was then purchased by the well-known potato business Albert Bartlett. In 2021, the celebrity chef James Martin joined forces with the business in order to re-brand it. It is now operating under the name of SpudULike by James Martin, with a new brand and logo. It has enabled the chef to create a range of new and appealing toppings for baked potatoes, including peri peri chicken wings, butter chicken and chickpea daal. The business has ten branches, mainly within large shopping malls.

Answer the following questions:
1. Why did SpudULike go into administration?
2. Who decided to join the business in 2021?
3. Would this situation with SpudULike be classed as a takeover, merger or joint venture?
4. Research the business using the following website: https://spudulikebyjamesmartin.com. Where can the branches be found?

Test yourself

1. What is external growth?
2. Why might a business decide to form a joint venture with another organisation?
3. Takeovers are quite common in the business world. Why is this?
4. Give an example of a takeover.
5. Write a definition of a merger.

5.1.3 Efficiencies and costs of business and enterprise expansion

Economies of scale

As a business grows, it benefits from a reduction in average costs of production. This reduction in costs is known as economies of scale and is what gives larger firms a competitive advantage over smaller firms. These economies can be split into different areas:

- Purchasing — As a business increases the size of its orders for raw materials or components, the cost to purchase each individual component falls. The business will have bulk discounts on larger orders. This reduces the average cost of production.
- Managerial — As businesses grow, they are able to employ specialist managers. These managers will know how to get the best value for each pound spent, whether it is in production, marketing or purchasing. This reduces the cost of output.
- Technical — As businesses grow, they are able to afford the latest equipment and to incorporate new methods of production. This again reduces average costs of output.
- Marketing — As a business grows, each pound spent on marketing has greater benefit for the business because it will become more widely known due to the marketing campaigns and materials that are produced.

- Financial — As businesses grow, they have access to a wider range of capital, which reduces the cost of borrowing for investment. Also, as assets grow, businesses are able to offer more security for borrowing, which reduces the risk to the lender and so reduces the cost of borrowing.

The largest businesses also often benefit from *external* economies of scale. These include the setting up of local suppliers to supply the goods and services required for the business to operate, often in competition with one another, reducing buying costs and allowing the use of systems such as JIT (see Section 4.1.2). Local colleges may also set up training schemes suited to the needs of the largest local employers, providing an available pool of skilled labour.

Diseconomies of scale

When diseconomies of scale appear, the average costs of production rise with output.

Diseconomies can be categorised into three different areas:

- Control — As a business grows and levels of hierarchy increase within the organisation, this can affect the control that individuals have within the business. The owners will have to learn to delegate tasks to others and trust that they will complete these tasks well for the business. If mistakes are made due to delegation, then this could cost the business in terms of time and orders.
- Co-ordination — Co-ordination is another crucial aspect of business. It is concerned with how the business can operate on a daily basis and be able to co-ordinate large numbers of staff, ensuring they are motivated and communicated with well. This is important as the business will continue to be successful with a good team of staff. Ineffective co-ordination could mean that orders are lost or completed inaccurately. Customers would then complain about the business, which would impact on its sales. The business would be advised in this situation to offer free replacements, which would affect its profits.
- Communication — As a business increases in size, the efficiency of communication can break down. This leads to increasing inefficiency and therefore increasing average costs. In larger businesses it may be harder to co-ordinate, satisfy and motivate workers, meaning they do not give of their best. This again means that as the business grows, the average output falls and average costs increase.

These diseconomies of scale are often qualitative in nature and so hard to measure financially. As businesses grow in size, they can become increasingly difficult to control as, for example, the business may need to deal with issues such as traffic congestion, the breakdown of relationships with suppliers and buyers, competition for labour and increasing employment costs.

Test yourself

1. Write a definition of economies of scale.
2. Explain what is meant by external economies of scale.
3. List and describe three different types of economies of scale.
4. Describe how diseconomies of scale affect organisations.

5.1.4 Challenges of growth

Whenever a business grows, there are a vast number of challenges. These can be categorised into four different areas:

- Additional physical resource requirements — These will include new buildings, equipment, technology and staff. Technology changes over time, which can be a large investment for a business and require maintenance throughout their lifetime with the business.
- Additional human resource requirements — A growing business may need to employ and train new staff. Existing staff may also require additional training to fulfil their roles. This will cost a business both financially and in terms of time.
- Sensitivities — Businesses need to be sensitive to local cultures and legislation. For example, there can be planning restrictions on building on greenfield sites and suggestions to do so by an expanding business can cause massive resentment in the local area. Any increase in size may cause increased traffic, pollution, etc. Businesses need to be mindful also of local culture and make sure that any changes are in keeping with the area.
- Understanding national and international legislation — If a business is to grow and operate internationally, it needs to have an understanding of the implications of this in terms of adhering to national and international legislation. Examples of legislation that it will need to understand include:
  - Import tariffs, which are a tax on imported goods and services. Tariffs will impact on demand for these products as they will make them more expensive to the business and to customers.
  - Import quotas, which are limits that are put on a business on the amount of products it can supply to a particular country. This will increase the price of the product as it is made rarer. For example, a country may limit the imports of particular brands of cars.

Remember

- Internal growth normally involves a business increasing in some form, for example expanding its product range.
- External growth involves increasing a business operation in size by merging with, taking over or becoming involved in a joint venture with another company.
- Merging two businesses means that the new organisation often becomes stronger in the competitive market, gaining more market share.
- Takeovers are not always welcomed by the businesses involved. Sometimes they can mean job losses for some employees.
- Efficiencies of business can have a positive or negative effect on the costs to a business.
- The challenges of growth must be considered and businesses must be sensitive to them while embracing the changes.

5 Business growth

Test yourself

1. How many categories of challenges of growth are there?
2. What is the difference between national and international legislation in terms of business?
3. Write a definition of import tariffs.
4. Write a definition of import quotas.

Practice questions

1. State the difference between a business updating a current product and developing a new product. [2 marks]
2. Identify the method of external growth from this explanation: 'When a business acquires control of another organisation.' [1 mark]
3. State **one** disadvantage of a takeover for a business. [1 mark]
4. Growth can be a challenge to a business. Explain **two** different challenges for a business caused by growth. [4 marks]

Assignment practice

Your sandwich and panini delivery business has been launched and has proved very popular, and after a year of trading you have decided to expand. For this, you will need to take on more staff and purchase another delivery van, which will have to be small and uniquely decorated.

Tasks:

1. By expandng your business, what challenges may you face? Create a document that identifies and explains these different challenges and how you will overcome them. (AO1, AO2, AO3)

2. How will economies and diseconomies of scale affect your business once it expands? (AO1, AO2)

Read about it

Brown, M. and Ellis, S. *Hacking Growth: How today's fastest-growing companies drive breakout success* (Virgin Digital, 2017) — Advice and guidance for businesses wanting to grow in a fast-changing business world.

Maslan, A. *Scale or Fail: How to build your dream team, explode your growth, and let your business soar* (Wiley, 2018) — Information regarding business growth.

www.tutor2u.net/business/blog/takeovers-and-mergers-the-language-of-ma#:~:text=Economies%20of%20scale,strategy%20of%20%E2%80%9Ccost%20leadership%E2%80%9D — Information regarding takeovers and mergers.

www.bbc.co.uk/news/business — Up-to-date news articles relating to business and the current economic climate.

www.gov.uk — Up-to-date information from the UK government, including key taxation details.

111

6 Sources of enterprise funding and business finance

About this content area

This content area focuses on how a business enterprise can gain its funding using a range of different methods. You will learn about:

- Business and enterprise funding — The various short-term and long-term funding types that businesses can access and the appropriateness of these for different legal structures.

- Financial terms, documents and tools — The different financial terms and how to calculate various financial formulae and documents. The relevance of these important calculations to the planning and monitoring of financial information for business enterprises.

6.1 Business and enterprise funding

Key term

Funding A method of gaining finance for a business.

The **funding** of any business or enterprise activity is an important aspect of business. As a business grows, the finances flowing in and out need to be understood and controlled since the amounts will get larger. Large organisations have employees who work within the Finance functional area who are experts in business finance, to ensure that the organisation's finances are kept in order. A business needs to be aware of the differences between the sources of short- and long-term funding that are available to it, as well as how these methods may be more appropriate to one legal business structure than another.

6.1.1 Funding types

Short-term funding

Companies often need to access finance to fund their business. A business may be in need of funding when it first starts as it may have to purchase or hire items to get up and running.

There are many different options for business funding, providing the financial circumstances and reasons for needing the money are suitable. Some may not be possible because of the situation a business is in, but other options will be available. Short-term funding is available to businesses for a short time, when they need money quickly. The money will usually need to be repaid within a short period of time, which is often less than one year. It is a short-term solution and can include the following examples.

6 Sources of enterprise funding and business finance

Trade credit
Trade credit is when credit is given to a business by its supplier for an agreed amount of time, such as 30, 60 or 90 days. The balance for the goods the business has had from the supplier must be paid within the agreed timescale. The business (which is known as 'trade') would be offered this credit by companies that it uses on a regular basis. An example would be a plumber who regularly buys materials from a specific supplier, which offers the plumber trade credit. A supplier will use this to encourage repeat custom.

Factoring
Factoring is when a third party buys a debt or invoice from a business for a discounted fee. The business receives the money, which is known as short-term funding, and the company that buys the debt also makes money from the fee. That company is then responsible for chasing the debt from the invoiced business. It is a short term solution for a business that may need a short term cash injection.

Overdraft
Overdrafts are a short-term source of finance. These are when a bank allows a business to withdraw money from its account, up to an agreed amount, even if it does not have the balance in its account. Any money withdrawn that was not in its account is then known as 'overdrawn'. Banks often charge their customers for having an overdraft option. Banks also set a limit on the overdraft that can be used, such as £200 per customer. For example, a business has £50 in its account and an agreed overdraft of £250. The business receives a bill for £75. It pays this bill, meaning its new balance is £25 overdrawn. (The business will be charged **interest** on its overdraft by the bank.) The business then receives £25 into its account. Its balance is now £0 as it has paid the overdrawn amount back to the bank.

Credit cards
Credit cards are provided by financial service businesses, such as banks. These days, many large retailers, such as Marks & Spencer and Sainsbury's, offer their own credit cards to customers. A credit card enables a customer to purchase items on credit. Each month, the customer is notified of the amount of credit that has been used. This amount should then be paid, otherwise **interest** will be added on to the amount owed each month. Sometimes companies offer an interest-free period of time when interest is not charged, but after this time interest will be incurred. A credit card is an expensive form of borrowing and should be used only as a short-term solution.

Long-term funding
Long-term funding requires a business to gain funds from an external source and repay the funding over a number of years. Having funding from a company will mean that you will have a long term association with

Activity
Tony is going to set up a mobile food van in his town centre. He plans to specialise in freshly made bagels, paninis, wraps and baguettes. He will also sell hot and cold drinks and freshly squeezed juices.
- In pairs, think about what equipment Tony will need in order to start his business. Share your ideas with the rest of your class.

Key term
Interest An amount of money that is added on to a loan and must be repaid by the customer.

the company who provide the funding to you. This is because the funding will have to be repaid in full.

Personal savings

Personal savings is money that the business owners have saved over the years to help fund their business. This method of funding is very easy to set up because, as the owner of the money, the individual can decide how much or how little is put into the business, and when. Using this method of funding is risky, however, because if the business fails, the money will be gone. This could put a strain on the owner and their family. It would always be advisable to keep an 'emergency fund', so that there are some savings left in case of this scenario.

Bank loan

A **loan** is an amount of money that is borrowed from a bank with an agreed payback date. The bank earns money, called interest, in return for lending the money to the business. The amount of interest charged to the customer is known as the **annual percentage rate (APR)**. Interest rates vary depending on the amount that is borrowed and the agreed time over which the loan will be repaid. The interest must be paid in addition to the loan amount. A bank loan can be classed as a medium- or long-term source of finance as the payments are spread over the term of the loan. The disadvantage of having a bank loan is that the interest charged can be expensive for the business. Depending on the size of the loan, the bank may ask for some security in case the loan is not repaid. Large assets, such as a house, are usually used for this purpose. If the loan is not repaid, the assets will be used (repossessed) against the loan.

> **Key terms**
>
> **Loan** A method of gaining finance from a financial institution. The loan must be repaid with interest within an agreed amount of time.
>
> **Annual percentage rate (APR)** The amount charged in interest to a customer who has taken out a loan.

> **Activity**
>
> Research how much it would cost to borrow £5000 for two years (24 months) home improvements from three different companies who provide loans. What are the differences in the interest rates they charge? How much in total will you repay over the period of the loan, including interest?
>
> Research the interest rates of three different credit cards. Work out how much interest you would pay if you borrowed £1000 over two years.

Leasing

Leasing means that a business can acquire a piece of equipment that it needs from a leasing company. The ownership of that product never passes to the business and always belongs to the leasing company. The business will benefit from the use of the equipment for the agreed period of the lease, at the end of which it will be returned to the leasing company. An example of this is a business that leases a 3D-printing machine for a new design of a product.

6 Sources of enterprise funding and business finance

Loan from family and friends
This is when a business is funded by friends and family of the owner. Like a bank loan, it is money that is borrowed for a period of time agreed by the parties involved. It would be advised to document the amounts involved and the agreed payback dates so that this does not cause any disagreements later. It is a risk borrowing from friends and family, as with any loan, because the finance still needs to be repaid even if the business fails.

Grants
Grants are a form of funding that is supported and funded by the government or other organisations, for example the Global Resilience Fund. Small businesses that meet specific criteria can apply for grants of between £500 and £500,000. New, developing and established small businesses may be eligible for grants. As well as offering access to business funding, the government or organisations will also offer support in the form of knowledge and expertise. During the pandemic, the government made several grants available to businesses to help them survive through the various lockdowns. The advantage of grants is that they do not need to be repaid.

Business angels
Business angels are individuals who have wealth and an entrepreneurial mind, who are willing to take risks in order to own a proportion of a business. They invest money in new business ventures in the hope that they will be successful. The popular BBC programme *Dragons' Den* is a good example of business angels (dragons) investing and taking risks by backing new businesses. The business angel will often have expertise in business and this could be useful to a new business. Some business angels want to be involved in the organisation, whereas others just want to invest. Either way, their investment means they will own part of the business and take a share of any profits made.

Crowdfunding
Crowdfunding involves many different people giving money, often for the purpose of starting a new business. People donate small amounts of money, normally online, which can generate publicity for the new project or business. Targets can be set and often are quickly achieved as awareness grows. There are different types of crowdfunding, including:

- Donation-based — When money is donated to a charity or a person, but the donor do not expect to get anything in return for their donation.
- Investment-based — When money is invested in a business and the investor receives something in return for their investment, perhaps a share of profits.
- Loan-based — When an amount of money is lent and the person receiving the money pays it back with interest to the lender.

> **Key term**
>
> **Crowdfunding** When many different people give money, often for the purpose of starting a new business.

Crowdfunding isn't regulated in the same way as bank loans, so there is a risk for the investors. Crowdfunding has become popular over the past few years. Recent reports state that tennis star Andy Murray now has a stake in at least 30 start-up businesses, focusing on his interests of sport, nutrition, dogs, and health and well-being, with the equity crowdfunding site Seedrs (source: www.growthcapitalventures.co.uk/insights/blog/7-british-celebrities-who-invest-in-startups).

Retained profit

Retained profit is profit made by the business that is invested back into the business rather than being distributed to the business's owners. It is often used to buy, expand or replace equipment or to pay for development activities that the business may have planned. It is only available to businesses that make a profit, so businesses that use this method are often well established. It does not cost the business anything as it is using its own money!

Share capital

Share capital is when a company sells shares in the business as a way to raise money. This means that the owners of the shares become shareholders (part-owners) in the business. In return for their investment, the shareholders will receive a dividend, which is a share of the profits made each year (if a profit is made).

Activity

Produce a leaflet for new businesses, detailing the different forms of funding that they could access. Using the internet, research some specific current deals for finance and use these as examples within your leaflet.

Key term

Share (owners') capital
When a company raises money by selling shares in the business, which gives the buyers a part-ownership of the business.

Remember

- There are different short-term and long-term funding options for businesses.
- Some financial institutions require security as part of any contract. Security is often a house or property asset.
- A business needs to carefully consider what form of financial funding will be manageable and appropriate.
- Interest rates vary according to the type of funding.
- Having an emergency fund of savings is important, in case anything goes wrong with the business.

Test yourself

1. What is the difference between short- and long-term funding?
2. Name four types of funding that a business could access and describe each one.
3. Why is it risky to fund a business using your personal savings?
4. What is the difference between an overdraft and a bank loan?
5. Write a definition of crowdfunding.
6. Explain retained profit and one advantage of this form of funding.

6.2 Financial terms, documents and tools

6.2.1 Financial terms and calculations

Once a business has been able to fund its operations, it must keep records of all its financial transactions.

Each year a business is required to produce an income statement. The income statement details the revenue (the money) that came into the business from the sales of products/services, as well as the expenses that the business had. Expenses are the money the business spent to make the products/services, such as the materials, the heat and light used within the business, the rent, etc. The income statement shows all this information in one document and then calculates the profit or loss the business made during the year. It enables a business to look at its performance during the year. A financial year is not the same as a calendar year — the financial year starts on 6 April and ends on 5 April the following year.

Sales revenue

Sales revenue is calculated by looking at the quantity of items sold multiplied by the selling price.

Sales revenue = Number of units sold × Price per unit

If a stationery shop sold 200 notebooks at £5 each, the calculation would be:

200 × £5 = £1000 sales revenue

Gross profit

Gross profit is the amount of profit made by a business after subtracting all the costs that are directly related to manufacturing and selling its products/services (its cost of sales). It is calculated in the following way:

Gross profit = Revenue – Cost of sales

If a business purchased a light for £40 but sold it for £90 to a customer, the gross profit would be calculated as:

£90 – £40 = £50 gross profit

Activity

Write down a list of expenses that you think a small milkshake business has. Compare your answers with the rest of your class.

Key terms

Sales revenue The amount of money that a business receives from selling goods and services. It is calculated by multiplying the quantity of items sold by the selling price.

Gross profit The difference between the money a business received from selling goods and services and the cost of making the products or services. It is calculated by subtracting the cost of sales from the sales revenue figure.

> **Key terms**
>
> **Net profit** A more accurate calculation of how the business is doing than gross profit, as it takes into account the costs that the business incurs. It is calculated by subtracting all expenses from the gross profit figure.
>
> **Break-even** The level of output at which total costs equal total revenue. This is the point at which a business makes no profit and no loss.

Net profit

Net profit is different from gross profit. The net profit is a more accurate calculation of how the business is doing as it takes into account all the costs that the business incurs, including wages of staff, heat and light that are needed within the business, etc. It is calculated in the following way:

Net profit = Gross profit – Cost of running the business

For example, if a business has a gross profit of £20,000 and running costs of £9000, to work out the net profit the calculation would be:

£20,000 – £9000 = £11,000 net profit

Break-even level of output

Break-even is the level of output at which total costs equal total revenue. This is the point at which a business makes no profit and no loss.

A business is able to calculate the number of sales it needs to make in order to break even each year. When a business calculates its break-even point, there are a number of assumptions that have to be made:

- That all output that has been made is sold.
- That there is no inventory (stock) left unsold.
- That only one type of product is made by the business.
- That all costs are categorised as either fixed costs or variable costs.

The break-even point can be calculated using either the break-even formula or a break-even graph.

Break-even formula

The formula for break-even is:

$$\text{Break-even point (in units)} = \frac{\text{Fixed costs}}{\text{Selling price per unit} - \text{Variable costs per unit}}$$

Contribution is the amount left over after variable costs have been subtracted from sales revenue. Contribution per unit is calculated as selling price per unit minus variable costs per unit. This means that the break-even formula can also be written as:

$$\text{Break-even point (in units)} = \frac{\text{Fixed costs}}{\text{Contribution per unit}}$$

Contribution is different from profit, as fixed costs are not subtracted from the selling price.

6 Sources of enterprise funding and business finance

Activity

Complete the table to calculate contribution per unit and break-even point in units. The first row has been completed as an example.

	Total fixed costs (£)	Selling price per unit (£)	Variable costs per unit (£)	Contribution per unit (£)	Break-even point in units
1	60,000	20	10	20 – 10 = 10	60,000 / 10 = 6000 units
2	240,000	100	60		
3	600,000	25	15		
4	500,000	36	11		
5	3,000,000	250	150		
6	500,000	500	300		
7	500,000	300	200		
8	300,000	250	150		
9	300,000	150	50		
10	900,000	450	200		

Case study

Snuffie Dog Apparel sells luxury dog collars and leads. The owner, Anjum, has prepared the following table of costs based on varying levels of output.

Output of collars and leads (units)	Variable costs per collar and lead (£)	Total variable costs (£)	Total fixed costs (£)	Total costs (£)
20,000	5	100,000 (20,000 × 5)	250,000	350,000 (100,000 + 250,000)
30,000	5		250,000	
50,000	5		250,000	
75,000	3		250,000	
90,000		270,000	250,000	
100,000	2.50		250,000	

Answer the following question:
1. You are required to help Anjum work out the missing figures. Complete the table. The first line has been completed for you.

NCFE Level 1/2 Technical Award in Business and Enterprise

> **Key terms**
>
> **Profit** The business owner's reward for investing in the business organisation.
>
> **Loss** Occurs when the total costs that the business has to pay are more than the revenue that the business earns from selling its products and services.
>
> **Margin of safety** A business will determine the amount sales that need to be made before the break even point is achieved which means that they are within the tolerated levels. This will mean that the business will not make a profit but also not make a loss.

Break-even graphs

It is also possible to calculate the break-even point and present it in a graph. For more on creating a break-even graph, see Section 6.2.3.

Profit and loss

Most businesses exist to make a profit. **Profit** is the business owner's reward for investing in the business organisation. A **loss** occurs when the total costs that the business has to pay are more than the revenue that the business earns from selling its products/services.

For example, if a business's total costs are £350 and its total revenue from sales is only £300, the business would make a loss of £50. If this continued, the business would continue to make a loss on these products/services, which would not be good for its long-term prospects.

Businesses often want to know how much profit a particular product/service is making. The calculation for this is:

Profit or loss per unit = Selling price (revenue) per unit − Total cost per unit

(Remember: Total cost per unit = Fixed costs per unit + Variable costs per unit)

The calculation to find out profit for a given level of output is:

Profit or loss = Sales revenue − Total costs

Margin of safety

Margin of safety is the number of sales that can fall before the break-even point is reached (meaning that the business makes no profit). The calculation also enables a business to calculate how many sales have to be made for a particular product/service. The calculation for this is:

Margin of safety = Actual sales − Break-even sales

For example, if a business has calculated a break-even point of 1000 products and it actually sells 1500, the margin of safety will be:

1500 − 1000 = 500 products

This means that the business is doing well as it has made sales of 500 above the break-even point, which will mean more profit for the business. If the margin of safety is below the break-even point, however, the business may have to consider if it is worth selling the specific product/service any longer as it will be making a loss.

> **Test yourself**
>
> 1. How do you calculate gross profit?
> 2. What is the difference between gross profit and net profit?
> 3. Write a definition of profit.
> 4. What is break-even?
> 5. How do you calculate the margin of safety?
> 6. If a business consistently makes a loss, what would you advise that it does?

6.2.2 Costs, liabilities and assets

Costs

It is importance for a business to keep financial records, as it ensures all the costs that are made or received by the business can be tracked and then documented. There are many different **costs** to a business throughout its life, from the very beginning, as it grows, if it changes direction or if it decides to end.

Start-up costs

When a business first starts, it will have start-up costs. These costs affect a new business because it has to purchase specific items before it can begin producing products or services. Think about the Activity on page 113 where you wrote a list of equipment Tony would need to set up a mobile food van and start trading. The purchase of these items would form part of his start-up costs.

The start-up costs for each business will be different as they depend on what the business is selling to its customers. If the new business offered a service, such as a vet, it would need premises, furniture, IT equipment and staff. A shop would have to purchase stock, have the right fixtures and fittings to display the goods, and have premises and IT equipment. A new manufacturer would have large costs for setting up a factory, such as machinery, equipment, tools and parts.

Fixed costs

Some of the running costs a business has to pay will not change; these are called **fixed costs**. These have to be paid every month, irrespective of whether the business has a good or a bad month of sales. Examples of fixed costs include:

- rent
- loan repayments
- advertising
- insurance, for example of the buildings and the building contents
- salaries
- utilities, for example electricity and water.

> **Key terms**
>
> **Costs** Financial costs that have to be paid in order for a business to function.
>
> **Fixed costs** Costs that do not change no matter how many products are produced, for example rent, loans, advertising and salaries.

Figure 6.1 Fixed costs

NCFE Level 1/2 Technical Award in Business and Enterprise

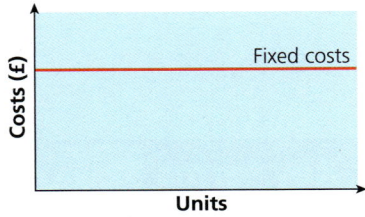

Figure 6.2 Graph of fixed costs

Remember that fixed costs do not change (increase or decrease) if the output from a business changes.

A graph of fixed costs would be a straight line, as shown in Figure 6.2.

Variable costs

Variable costs change according to a business's level of output. For example, if 50 items are made and then another 20 are needed, the business will need to order in more materials to make the products. The raw materials and manpower that are used to make the extra output are examples of variable costs. Other examples of variable costs include:

- Stock — Also known as inventory. This is the goods or items that a business keeps in its shop or warehouse for sale to its customers. For example, a sandwich shop may have stock of bags of crisps and bottles of drink.
- Components — These are the parts that make up a whole item. For example, flour would be a component in making a bread roll.
- Packaging costs — These are the costs of packaging the finished products. For example, the costs of putting sandwiches into boxes ready for sale.

> **Key term**
>
> **Variable costs** Costs that vary directly with the level of output, for example stock, raw materials and packaging costs.

In a clothes factory, if production of clothing doubles, then the variable costs double; if production of clothing halves, the variable costs halve; if output is zero, then no variable costs are incurred. A graph of variable costs would be a diagonal line, as shown in Figure 6.3.

Total variable costs = Variable costs per unit × Output level

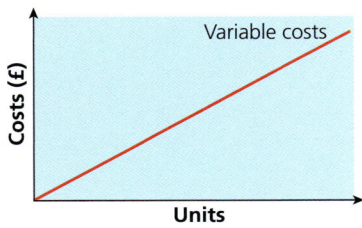

Figure 6.3 Variable costs

Activity

Aaliyah sells ice lollies in the summer at an outdoor swimming pool. On a busy day she can sell up to 300 lollies, each for £1.50. Her total revenue on a busy day when she sells out of lollies is: 300 × £1.50. Therefore, her total revenue is: £450.

Aaliyah has to pay £20 in rent each day that she sells her lollies at the pool. She works six days a week. The rent covers the electricity needed to keep the lollies frozen. This cost does not change, so on days when there are not that many people swimming, she makes fewer sales but still has to pay the £20 rent.

- Identify the fixed costs in the above case study.
- How much does Aaliyah pay each week for her fixed costs? Calculate this total.
- The swimming pool has decided to charge Aaliyah a weekly rent of £150 instead of a daily rate. It is also going to charge her a daily electricity charge, as there have been recent increases to this cost. This charge will be £3.00 per day. Aaliyah will be at the swimming pool six days a week and will have one day off. She will employ her brother, Ali, to cover her day off. Ali will be paid £45 for the day. How much will she now have to pay for her fixed costs?

6 Sources of enterprise funding and business finance

Liabilities

Liabilities are the debts that a business may have incurred while trading. It is not unusual for businesses to have liabilities, as they cannot own everything unless they have an endless supply of money! Some liabilities are short-term, for example a builder may have 60 days to repay the credit for building materials purchased. These short-term liabilities/debts are known as **current liabilities**.

Long-term (non-current) liabilities are debts that take much longer to pay, such as a bank loan or mortgage. Long-term liabilities are debts that will take more than 12 months to pay off.

Assets

Assets are the different resources that a business owns so that it can operate. Have you ever heard the expression 'You're a real asset'? It means that you add value, just like an asset in business terms. Like liabilities, assets fall into two separate categories:

- Non-current (fixed) assets are resources that are used again and again to help the business function and survive. Examples would be machinery, vehicles and premises.
- Current assets are items that can be quickly turned into cash, if required. Examples could be the business's stock (products that are already made that can be sold), the cash the organisation has in the bank, and the individuals or businesses that owe the company money (known as its debtors). An example of a debtor is shown in Figure 6.4, which shows that Company A has not paid for the products it has purchased from Company B.

> **Key terms**
>
> **Liabilities** Debts that a business may have incurred while trading.
>
> **Current liabilities** Short-term debts the business has that will need to be paid back within a year.
>
> **Non-current liabilities** Long-term debts that the business will have, such as a loan for machinery that helps the business with efficiency, which will take longer than a year to pay back.
>
> **Assets** Resources that a business owns so that it can operate.

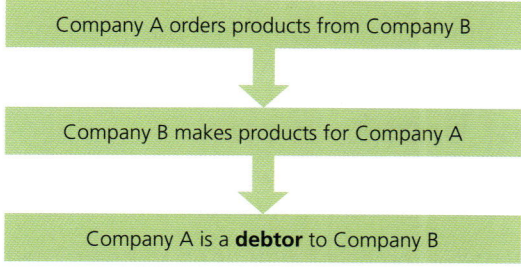

Figure 6.4 How a company can become a debtor

Test yourself

1. Are fixed costs and start-up costs the same? Explain your answer.
2. True or false? Paying the rent for premises is an example of a variable cost.
3. Give an example of a start-up cost.
4. What is the difference between liabilities and assets?
5. What are the two different types of liabilities?
6. Would a two-year bank loan be a current liability or a non-current (long-term) liability?
7. Write a definition of a variable cost.
8. Identify three different forms of fixed costs.

6.2.3 Financial documents

We have established the importance of businesses keeping good records of all financial transactions. These can be used to analyse the business's performance and make adjustments to the way that it operates. For example, if sales are slow during the summer months, more advertising could take place, with special introductory customer discounts given to try to generate more sales.

Break-even

We saw in Section 6.2.1 details about break-even, the point at which a business makes no profit or loss. A new business will often struggle to make a profit in its first years of trading, therefore new organisations usually aim to break even. This means that the business makes no profit or loss, but it is able to cover its costs so is not losing money. The owner of the business will need to review the business's costs and revenues on a regular basis, as these can fluctuate. This was highlighted in the pandemic, when the costs of various items (for example wheat, maize and soybeans, as well as animal feed) changed due to the demand, pushing up the cost of meat for consumers.

To recap:

- Costs — These are expenses that the business incurs when producing and selling its products and services.
- Revenue — This is the money that the business earns from selling its goods or services.
- Total revenue — This is the selling price of the goods that a business sells multiplied by the number of goods sold.
- Profit — This is the financial gain that a business makes. It is calculated as the difference between total revenue and total costs.

Definition of break-even

Break-even is the level of output at which total costs equal total revenue. At this point, a business is making no profit and no loss.

To work out the break-even point, you need to know the following costs:

- Fixed costs
- Variable costs per unit
- Selling price per unit

The break-even formula is:

$$\text{Break-even point (in units)} = \frac{\text{Fixed costs}}{\text{Selling price per unit} - \text{Variable costs per unit}}$$

For example, a local charity band wants to encourage people to download its latest music release. It needs to work out the break-even point so it knows when it will be making a profit, which it will then donate to its chosen charity. Its fixed costs are £600; the selling price per unit is 35p; the variable costs per unit are 20p. The calculation is:

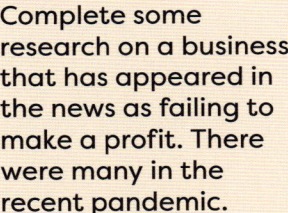

Activity

Complete some research on a business that has appeared in the news as failing to make a profit. There were many in the recent pandemic.

- In small groups, discuss strategies that the business could have introduced to increase its profit.

6 Sources of enterprise funding and business finance

Break-even point = £600 / (35p − 20p)

= £600 / 15p

= 4000 downloads before it breaks even

Activity

Using the break-even point formula, complete the following table to calculate the break-even point of various stationery items.

	Pens	Books	Pencils	Folders	Staplers
Fixed costs	£45,000	£100,000	£20,000	£10,000	£50,000
Price per unit	£2.00	£15.00	£1.00	£3.00	£4.00
Variable costs per unit	£0.50	£7.00	£0.20	£1.00	£1.50
Break-even point					

- If the fixed costs were to increase by 10% for each item, what do you think would happen to the break-even points?
- Why might a business's fixed costs increase?

Break-even chart 1

Some businesses like to present their break-even point in graphical form, known as a break-even chart. A break-even chart shows the lines of fixed costs, total costs and total revenue for each product/service. When drawing a break-even graph, three lines need to be plotted and drawn:

- Fixed costs
- Total costs
- Total revenue

The break-even point is the point at which the total revenue and total costs lines cross.

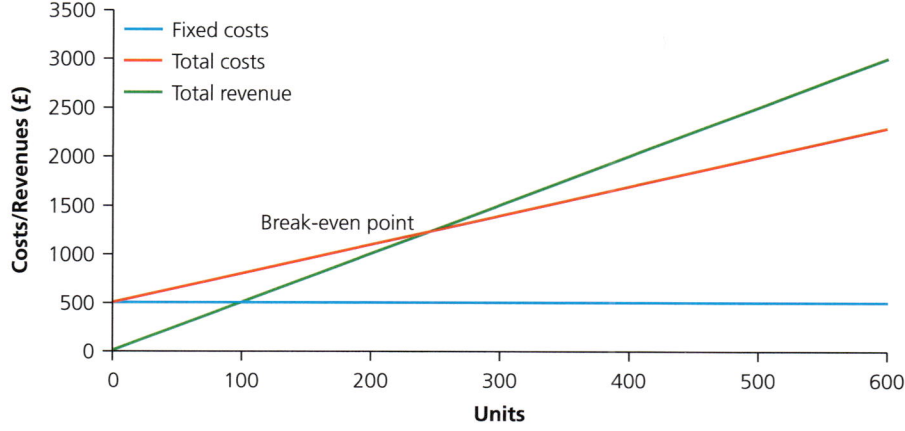

Figure 6.5 Break-even chart 1

On the horizontal axis, you will see that the number of units is shown. The vertical axis represents the costs and revenues.

The total revenue line shows the revenue the business will make at different levels of output/sales. This line will always start at zero because if the business sells nothing, then the revenue that it will make will be zero too! It is based on both the level of output and the selling price of this output.

The fixed costs line on the graph is a straight horizontal line because costs remain unchanged as the output/sales level changes. It does not matter what level of output the firm produces (even zero output makes no difference); any fixed costs will remain the same.

The total costs line will start at the same point as the fixed costs line. Total costs are calculated by adding fixed costs to variable costs.

Break-even chart 2

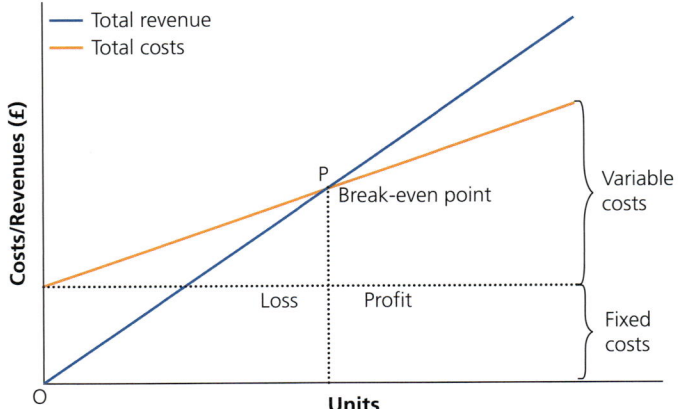

Figure 6.6 Break-even chart 2

Break-even point is when the total revenue and total costs lines meet and cross over. There is a small dotted line in Figure 6.6 to demonstrate this cross. All sales above this point will make a profit and anything below it will make a loss for the business.

If variable costs vary directly, this means that the total variable costs are totally dependent on the level of output. If output doubles, then the variable costs would double. If output halves, the variable costs would halve. If output was zero, then no variable costs would be incurred. An example can be seen in Figure 6.7.

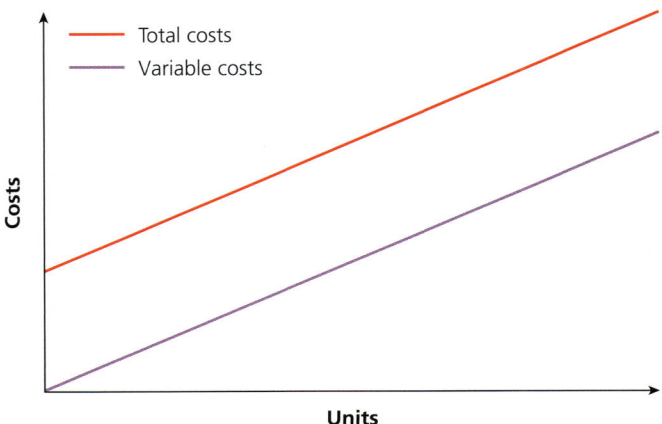

Figure 6.7 Impact of variable costs on total costs

6 Sources of enterprise funding and business finance

Activity

Look at the following graph and mark on the break-even point.

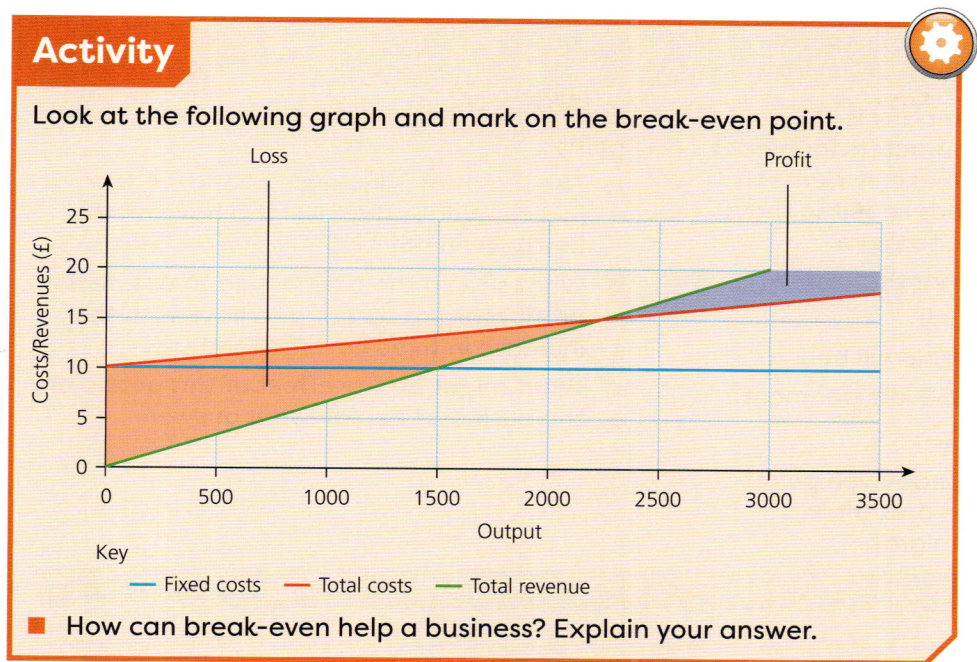

- How can break-even help a business? Explain your answer.

Activity

Bailey Brown makes small garden tables. His fixed costs are £20,000 and variable costs are £10 per unit. The selling price for each unit is £60. His aim is to break even as quickly as possible.

The table below shows how Bailey can work out his break-even point.

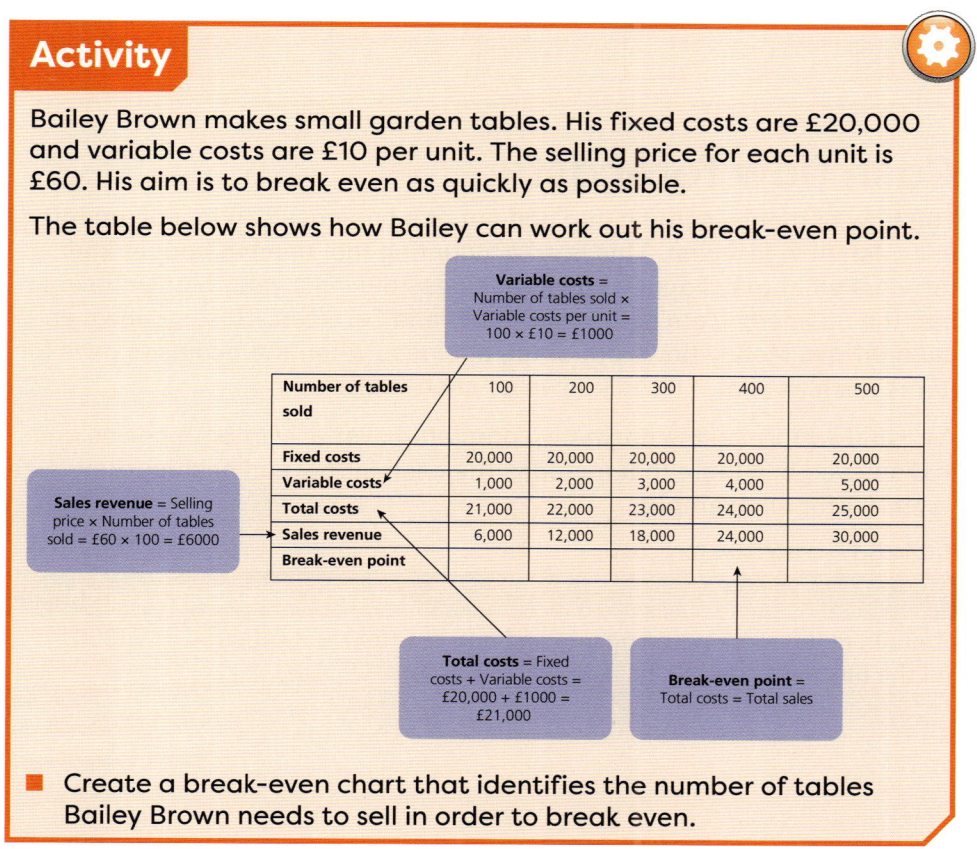

Variable costs = Number of tables sold × Variable costs per unit = 100 × £10 = £1000

Sales revenue = Selling price × Number of tables sold = £60 × 100 = £6000

Total costs = Fixed costs + Variable costs = £20,000 + £1000 = £21,000

Break-even point = Total costs = Total sales

Number of tables sold	100	200	300	400	500
Fixed costs	20,000	20,000	20,000	20,000	20,000
Variable costs	1,000	2,000	3,000	4,000	5,000
Total costs	21,000	22,000	23,000	24,000	25,000
Sales revenue	6,000	12,000	18,000	24,000	30,000
Break-even point					

- Create a break-even chart that identifies the number of tables Bailey Brown needs to sell in order to break even.

NCFE Level 1/2 Technical Award in Business and Enterprise

Case study

A retro adventure gaming company is producing model kits of its characters for model enthusiasts to purchase and make. It wants to work out how many kits it needs to sell so that it can set its sales team realistic targets.

- Fixed costs are £800 per month.
- Variable costs are £4 per unit.
- Selling price of each model kit will be £20.
- It thinks that it might sell 150 kits per month.

Answer the following questions:

1. Work out the company's break-even point using the table below, then present this information in a break-even graph.
2. Explain how you worked out the break-even point.
3. a. The fixed costs increase by £100 each month. What effect will this have on the break-even point?
   b. What should the business do to ensure its profit margins do not decrease with the increase in fixed costs?
   c. What might be the effect of this action on the business? Explain your answer.

Number of kits	0	25	50	75	100	125	150
Fixed costs							
Variable costs							
Total costs							
Sales revenue							

Key terms

Cash inflow Money that is coming into the business.

Cash outflow Money that is going out of the business.

Cash flow forecast

The flow of money coming into and out of a business can be documented in a cash flow forecast. This is an accounting tool used to budget and forecast what may happen with a business during a year. Money flows into the business from selling products and services. This is known as **cash inflow**. Money flows out of the business when the business pays for items such as rent. This is known as **cash outflow**.

A cash flow forecast is normally completed over a 12-month period and is displayed in a table that includes the cash inflow and cash outflow. See Table 6.1 for an example.

Table 6.1 A cash flow forecast

	January	February	March	...
Details of the money coming into and out of the business	£1000	£1000	£1000	
...				

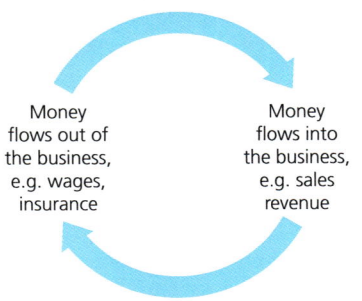

Figure 6.8 Money flowing into and out of a business

Money flows out of the business, e.g. wages, insurance

Money flows into the business, e.g. sales revenue

6 Sources of enterprise funding and business finance

The cash flow forecast is used by businesses to identify issues that may occur, hopefully before they happen, and to plan for future projects, such as expanding the business using the finance from profits. If the business identifies issues that may occur, it can try to avoid these by planning ahead. An example could be increasing sales in busy periods to cover the times when sales are lower, or reducing the business's costs each month.

For example, The T-shirt Company has started to compile a cash flow forecast, shown in Figure 6.9. It is a local family-run business that would like to expand its operations in the next five years, so this document is very useful for its planning.

	Jan (£)	Feb (£)	Mar (£)
Opening balance	10,000	62,800	134,100
Cash inflows			
Sales revenue	60,000	65,000	70,000
Loan	5,000	5,000	5,000
Sale of van		14,000	
Total cash inflows	65,000	84,000	75,000
Cash outflows			
Materials	3,000	3,500	4,000
Wages	8,000	8,000	8,000
Rent	1,000	1,000	1,000
Other expenses	200	200	200
Total cash outflows	12,200	12,700	13,200
Net cash flow	52,800	71,300	61,800
Closing balance	62,800	134,100	195,500

Opening balance is the amount of money that a business has at the start of the month

Total cash inflows is the amount of money that the business expects to receive during the month

Total cash outflows is the amount of cash that the business expects to pay out in the month

Net cash flow is the difference between the money coming into and out of the business: £65,000 – £12,200 = £52,800

Closing balance is worked out by adding the opening balance figure to the net cash flow figure. The closing balance is £10,000 + £52,800 = £62,800. This figure then becomes the opening balance for the next month

Figure 6.9 The T-shirt Company's cash flow forecast

The **opening balance** is the amount of money that a business has when it first starts to operate. It is important to have an opening balance so that equipment can be purchased and so that bills can be paid, including paying staff and suppliers that make the products/services. The opening balance is the amount of cash a business has at the start of the year.

The **closing balance** is the money that the business has at the end of the financial year. This balance will take into consideration the amounts that the business has had to pay as well as the money that the business has generated throughout the year by selling its goods and services.

Key terms

Net cash flow The total inflow received minus the cash outflows.

Opening balance The amount of cash a business has at the start of the year.

Closing balance The amount of cash a business has at the end of the year.

NCFE Level 1/2 Technical Award in Business and Enterprise

Activity

Now you have had a chance to look at some cash flow forecasts, create your own using the following information.

Shaena and Neve have a dance business called Strz Academy, which is popular with boys and girls aged 6 to 16. They offer a range of different dance lessons after school, at weekends and during the holidays. They are producing a cash flow forecast for the first five months of the year and have asked for your help. The following figures are a forecast.

They have an opening balance of £2500. The inflow into the business will be in the form of sales, which they have estimated will be:

- January £4600
- February £6700
- March £7300
- April £3600
- May £8000

They have several outflows from the business:

- Materials for the classes and shows that the students participate in. These vary each month but they predict costs will be: January £1500; February £1800; March £2200; April £1400; May £2500.
- Wages change according to the staff that are needed, but they have estimated that these will be: January £1800; February, March and May £3000; April £2500.
- They will produce marketing for the business, with costs being: January £60; February £10; March and May £50; April £30.
- The business has other overheads, which are predicted to be: January £120; February £40; March and May £50; April £130.

Tasks:

1. Create your cash flow forecast in a table.
2. Calculate the cash inflows and outflows as well as the opening and closing balances for each month.
3. Some figures are negative. What does that mean for a business?
4. What is the opening balance for January?
5. What is the total outflow figure for March?
6. What is the closing balance figure for April?
7. What is the closing balance for May?
8. How much more cash could the business have from the first opening balance to the last closing balance in May?

Income statement

We looked at income statements in Section 6.2.1. An income statement is presented in a particular way. The layout is important for the business, as it must be simple and show the sales and expenses, as well as the gross profit and net profit. For example, Party Plus produces a wide variety of products for any celebration, from birthdays to Easter, Eid, Christmas, etc. Each year it produces an income statement that details the profit or loss made.

6 Sources of enterprise funding and business finance

Income statement for Party Plus

	£
Sales revenue	175,400
Less costs of sales	97,700
Gross profit	**77,700**
Less expenses	48,200
Net profit	**29,500**

Figure 6.10 Party Plus's income statement

This basic income statement shows that Party Plus's sales revenue was £175,400, meaning that it sold this value of goods over the year. It can only know this by keeping receipts and records of each sale. The **cost of sales** on the income statement is the amount that it cost the business to make all of the products it produced and sold. These costs include the materials to make the products. The cost of sales is deducted from the sales revenue, which then displays the gross profit, which for Party Plus is £77,700. Gross profit is the profit before **expenses** are taken off the total, and is the first main figure shown on the income statement.

The next part of the income statement is where the expenses are added up and then deducted from the gross profit. As Figure 6.10 is a basic example of an income statement, a total figure of £48,200 is shown for expenses. More detailed income statements detail what specific expenses could be, such as rent, wages/salaries, etc. (see Figure 6.11). The expenses are then deducted from the gross profit to give the business's overall net profit figure. This is the money that the business has access to after all costs and expenses have been deducted. This shows the business how much profit it has earned during the financial year and it can then decide what to do with this profit.

Having an income statement means that a business can compare these calculations over time and analyse the changes in revenue and expenses. This allows it to alter its business methods accordingly. For Party Plus, for example, if the costs of making bunting increased, this cost may have to be passed on to customers through increased prices. This may affect sales, so Party Plus may consider changing to a cheaper form of materials to produce the bunting. Collating its sales revenue allows Party Plus to identify which products were the most and least popular. It may use this to decide to change the types of products it stocks or to advertise particular products more prominently to try and increase sales.

> **Key terms**
>
> **Cost of sales** The costs to a business from making products/services, such as materials.
>
> **Expenses** The costs that the business incurs on a day-to-day basis while operating.

NCFE Level 1/2 Technical Award in Business and Enterprise

Gross profit is calculated by using the sales revenue figure and subtracting from this the cost of sales.

The gross profit for Hot Drinks For You is £57,000.

Income statement for Hot Drinks For You

	£	£
Sales revenue		175,400
Less costs of sales		53,000
Gross profit		**57,000**
Less expenses:		
Salaries	12,300	
Rent	5,600	
Vehicles	4,000	
Repairs and maintenance	1,000	
		22,900
Net profit		**34,100**

Net profit is calculated by taking the gross profit figure and subtracting from this the total expenses figure.

The net profit for Hot Drinks For You is £34,100.

Figure 6.11 An income statement for Hot Drinks For You

Activity

Financial information about a business is given below.

- Sales £156,400
- Cost of sales £80,200
- Rent £20,000
- Advertising £7000
- Equipment £150
- Uniforms £100
- General expenses £7000
- Computers £300

Tasks:
1 Prepare an income statement for the owner of the business.
2 What is the gross profit?
3 What items could be included in the business's general expenses?
4 What is the business's net profit?

6 Sources of enterprise funding and business finance

Statement of financial position (balance sheet)

A statement of financial position (also called a balance sheet) gives a snapshot of a business's assets and liabilities at a particular point in the financial year. This tells the business how much it is worth. There are three main parts:

- Section 1: The assets
- Section 2: The liabilities
- Section 3: The capital and reserves that the business may or may not have.

These documents are accessed by stakeholders in the business. People who have a vested interest in the performance of the organisation, for example shareholders, banks or employees, might be interested to see how the business is doing. A statement of financial position should balance, as the value of a business's assets is exactly the same as its liabilities and capital added together. If it does not balance then there is a problem.

See the example in Figure 6.12 for Fans Limited.

> **Key term**
>
> **Non-current (fixed) assets** Show the value of significant purchases that a business has that help run the business, such as machinery, technology or transport.

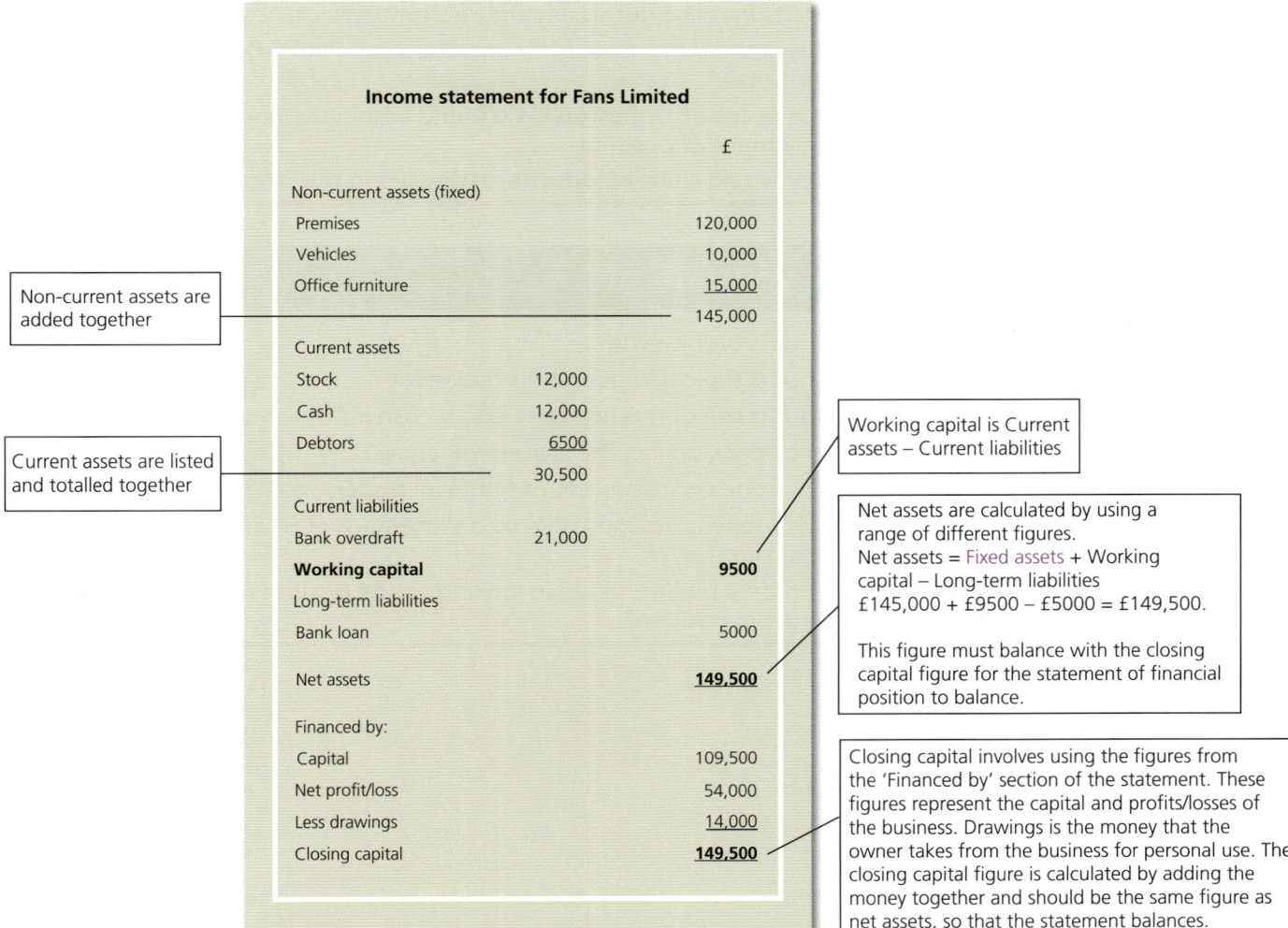

Figure 6.12 A statement of financial position

Activity

Balance is a small business that specialises in fitness. It has been operating for two years, during which time the business has grown.

Fixed assets	Current assets	Current liabilities	Long-term liabilities
Premises £1000	Stock £450	Creditors £440	Bank loan £100
Fixtures and fittings £670	Debtors £156		Capital £1012
	Cash £76		Profit £900
			Less drawings £100

- Using the figures above, prepare a statement of financial position for Balance, remembering that it should balance!

  Net assets = Fixed assets + Current assets − Current liabilities − Long-term liabilities

- What does the net assets figure show us?
- Why is the statement of financial position document useful to a business?
- True or false? Debtors will be found within the capital section of the statement of position.
- Why would shareholders be interested in this document?

Test yourself

1. What is break-even?
2. What is the calculation for break-even?
3. What is the difference between a cash inflow and a cash outflow?
4. What does an income statement show?
5. What does a statement of financial position tell a business?
6. How many parts are there to a statement of financial position and what are they?
7. Who may be interested in looking at the business's statement of financial position?

6 Sources of enterprise funding and business finance

6.2.4 Ratio analysis

Ratios enable a business to judge if it is performing to the expected level, or is below or outperforming expectations. Over time, the figures can be analysed and trends identified that can be used when planning for future years. However, ratios do have limitations. While they can identify where performance is good or poor, they do not give the reasons why. They are also not useful for seasonal businesses as they do not take into account the time of year. (This information would be in a cash flow forecast.)

The business's managers will use the ratios to look at past results to decide how to control the business and plan for the future. Ratios are also useful for individuals and organisations who have a vested interest in the business. Any person who is interested in investing in the business will want to see these figures, to help them decide if the business is worth investing in. Banks that have loaned the business money will use the figures to decide if the business will be able to afford to repay the loan or if it is a risk.

There are two main forms of ratio analysis that you will need to calculate and understand: profitability ratios and liquidity ratios.

Profitability ratios

Profitability ratios involve looking specifically at whether a business has the capacity to make a profit. The main ratios that are used are net profit margin and return on capital employed.

Net profit margin

The net profit margin ratio involves the net profit figure and the sales revenue. It is displayed as a percentage. The higher the percentage a business achieves, the better, as a higher number shows it is making more profit.

$$\text{Net profit margin} = \frac{\text{Net profit}}{\text{Sales revenue}} \times 100$$

For example:

$$\frac{£4000}{£80{,}000} \times 100 = 5\%$$

This means that for every £1 of goods the business sells, it makes 5% net profit, which is 5p.

A business will want its net profit ratio to keep increasing, year on year, because this shows that its profits, losses and expenses are being controlled within the correct levels, so it can continue to grow. If any reductions occur, such as the margin reducing, the reasons should be investigated. It could be, for example, that the business had to employ extra staff or increase its advertising because it launched a new product or service, and this increased its expenses.

> **Key term**
>
> **Ratios** Calculations that enable a business to judge how it is performing.

> **Activity**
>
> In pairs, select a large business that is based within your local town. Identify four groups of users who would be interested in the analysis of this business's ratios. Discuss why you think these groups are relevant.
> - Share your ideas with the rest of your class.

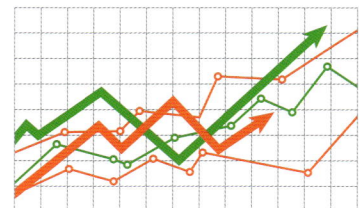

Figure 6.13 Business performance

Return on capital employed

The return on capital employed (ROCE) ratio is a calculation that shows a business's profit compared to the capital the owners have invested into the business. It is an important ratio, as it measures how the business is performing in its sector. The higher the ratio, the better the business is performing. If its ROCE figure reduces, a business would be advised to investigate why this has occurred. It could be a sector-wide reduction.

For example, if a bookshop's ROCE increased by 5% from one year to another while other bookshops' ROCE reduced by 5%, then investors can see that this is good in comparison to its competitors.

$$\text{Return on capital employed} = \frac{\text{Profit before tax and interest}}{\text{Long-term capital employed}} \times 100$$

For example:

$$\frac{£120,000}{£599,000} \times 100 = 20\%$$

This figure shows what the company gets back for the money it invests, so in the above case it gets 20% back in profits. The higher the percentage, the better for a business.

Liquidity ratios

Liquidity ratios enable a business to determine if it is able to pay its bills. They focus on the business's **current assets** and current liabilities. The two main ratios that are used are current ratio and acid-test ratio.

Current ratio

The current ratio focuses on how much working capital a business has, meaning its liquid resources that cover its running costs (such as paying bills). Remember, if a business is short of working capital, it may have cash flow problems and would need to address this.

$$\text{Current ratio} = \frac{\text{Current assets}}{\text{Current liabilities}}$$

For example:

$$\frac{£34,000}{£21,000} = £1.62 : 1$$

The above answer shows that there is £1.62 of current assets. This is given as a ratio in relation to £1 of current liabilities, so is written as 1.62 : 1. This ratio enables a business to judge its performance. The ratio in the example is positive, meaning the business can cover its costs. Businesses in general want to aim for a current ratio of 2 : 1, meaning £2 of current assets to every £1 of current liabilities.

The ratio, however, will be determined by the business sector. For example, internet-based businesses have different current ratios to high street shops. This is because internet sales have increased year on year for several years, resulting in several large high street businesses ceasing trading as they were not as relevant. If a business's current ratio figure is below 2 : 1, it could show that the organisation has inadequate

> **Key term**
>
> **Current assets** Items that the business has that are cash or near-cash, such as stock, money owed to it and cash that is in the bank.

6 Sources of enterprise funding and business finance

levels of working capital. A business that has a high current ratio should consider investing the money into other opportunities.

Acid-test ratio

The acid-test ratio uses the current assets and current liabilities, which can be found on the statement of financial position. Businesses aim for a ratio of 1 : 1, as this shows the organisation is able to pay its current liabilities from its liquid assets.

As with the current ratio, the acid-test ratio depends on the sector the business operates in, as some sectors enable an organisation to operate with a lower acid-test ratio than others. For example, businesses in the technology industry may have times when their acid-test ratios are very high because of high sales due to new products. For this industry, it can be difficult to balance investment into new technological developments to the sales of products. In the construction sector, a business may appear to be positive but it often takes time for accounts to be settled, which impacts on the performance of the business. A construction company would need to be aware of this.

Activity

An IT consultancy business wants to work out its current ratio as well as its acid-test ratio. Use the following figures to calculate its current and acid-test ratios:
- Current assets = £500,000
- Stock = £25,000
- Current liabilities = £310,000

$$\text{Acid-test ratio} = \frac{\text{Current assets less stock (closing inventory)}}{\text{Current liabilities}}$$

For example:

$$\frac{£81,000}{£75,000} = £1.08 : 1$$

6.2.5 Cash flow management

The importance of cash to business and enterprise

Managing a business's **cash flow** is an important aspect of financial control. We learned in Section 6.2.3 about the cash flow forecast and how this is calculated. This important document can show an organisation if it will have enough cash in the future to keep running the company, as well as ensuring that the business owners plan for the future. Businesses evolve over time and having such information enables the owners to look at the financial evidence of how the organisation is performing. This could be presented to future investors or financial institutions that may be approached to invest in or loan money to the business.

Key term

Cash flow Shows a business if it will have enough cash in the future to keep running, as well as ensuring that the business owners plan for the future.

The usefulness of cash flow forecasting to business and enterprise

Cash flow can limit a business, as an estimate of how it will perform in the year ahead could result in incorrect assumptions being made by managers, for example regarding sales. If a business is reliant on the summer weather (for example a deckchair-hire business) and the weather is poor, its estimates of sales could be inaccurate. Weather cannot be predicted but it can have a direct impact on the cash flow of a

137

business. Other impacts could be the economy or competition from other businesses. An increase in the minimum wage, for example, will affect all businesses and may adversely affect cash flow.

In the Activity on the left, you identified what a person may have to do to plan a birthday celebration, as well as a business planning the launch of a new product. Planning is key in both these situations, and it is the same for a business that wants to improve its cash flow position. Ideas that a business may use include:

- A company would be advised to ensure that all debtors are regularly paying bills owed to the business. If these debtors are chased and the balances are paid, this will have an immediate positive impact as these payments will now be part of the business. It is important for the business to know what cash it has available.
- A business may also want to consider reducing the amount of credit that it gives to other businesses, meaning reducing the amount of goods that another business can purchase on credit and pay for at a later date. This will also have a positive impact on the business's cash flow. However, other businesses may look elsewhere for a business that will give them more credit.

Solutions to cash flow problems

- A business will have to look at its cash outflows. It could request to delay paying any trade payments until others have settled their accounts with it. This means that if the organisation has purchased goods from Business A, it could ask Business A for an extension to settle the account until it has received payment from Business B. It could also ask Business A if it could pay off the goods over a longer time period, as this would reduce its cash outflows.
- A business could delay purchasing non-essential items, such as machinery or vehicles, until its cash flow is more fluid. At times, organisations have to reduce their spending to enable their savings to recover. Delaying the purchase of assets is a method of reducing outflows.
- A business may also need to reduce the wages and salaries of its employees, or even the number of staff it employs. This would be very unpopular with staff, but if the business could work with a reduced number of staff, this would be more economical and could enable the business to be more efficient.

Businesses should be encouraged to have a contingency fund built into their cash flow forecasts. This means that if unseen circumstances occur, these can be covered by the extra fund that has been saved by the business. If businesses do not have a contingency fund, they may choose to seek additional sources of finance if cash flow issues occur. Options could be getting a loan from a bank or setting up an overdraft facility as a short-term solution. For more on short-term funding, see Section 6.1.1.

A business may also choose to enter into a hire-purchase agreement. This is when it hires a piece of equipment or machinery for an agreed

Activity

You are planning a party for a relative who has an important birthday this year.

- Write down a list of things that will be required to ensure that they have a memorable night of celebrations with friends and family. With a partner, devise some ideas for how you might budget for this celebration.
- In the same pairs, consider how a business may budget for the launch of a new product or service. What might the business need to do in order to ensure the launch is successful?
- Share your ideas with the rest of your class.

6 Sources of enterprise funding and business finance

time period, paying for its use during this time. At the end of the agreement, the business has the opportunity to purchase the item or to give it back. This is why it is called hire purchase, as the item is hired with the option of purchasing it.

Case study

Sarah Khan started a successful sandwich delivery business five years ago, as she saw a gap in the market. Her customers work on business parks and she and her team provide sandwich lunches directly to businesses using a pre-order service. Sarah has worked hard to produce all the required accounting documents to enable her to track her finances. She has noticed over the past six months that her sales have started to decrease. This is impacting on her cash flow and she is now having to consider what to do next in order to keep operating.

Answer the following question:

1 Write an email to Sarah explaining how she could investigate exactly when and why her sales started to reduce, and also what she could do to improve her cash flow management.

Remember

- Start-up costs are the costs that are incurred when a business first starts.
- Liabilities are debts the business has; assets are the different resources that the business owns.
- Fixed costs remain the same, whereas variable costs change with the level of output.
- Break-even can focus a business on the output it needs to sell in order for all costs to be covered before profit is made.
- The break-even formula is:

$$\text{Break-even point (in units)} = \frac{\text{Fixed costs}}{\text{Selling price per unit} - \text{Variable cost per unit}}$$

- The performance of a business can be measured using ratios, but it is important to consider the sector that the business operates in when using these ratios to assess the financial position of the business against its competition.
- The income statement details the revenue (money) that comes into the business from the sales of products/services, as well as the expenses that the business has used.
- A statement of financial position is a useful document for a business to compile, as it gives a snapshot of the company's assets and liabilities at a particular point in the financial year. This tells the company how much it is worth. The statement of financial position might also be called the balance sheet.
- A cash flow forecast is a prediction of what may happen within a year for a business and is used for cash flow management.
- Ratios enable a business to determine how it is performing, which could highlight positive or negative issues.

Test yourself

1 What is the purpose of a cash flow forecast?
2 Identify two cash inflows to a business.
3 Identify three cash outflows from a business.
4 How do ratios impact on a business?

NCFE Level 1/2 Technical Award in Business and Enterprise

Read about it

https://entrepreneurhandbook.co.uk/grants-loans — Details of the different types of grants available to businesses.

www.simplecrowdfunding.co.uk/news/what-is-crowdfunding — Information on the different aspects of crowdfunding.

www.bbc.com/bitesize/guides/zhm6sbk/revision/1 — Revision materials looking at financial records.

www.tutor2u.net/business/reference/finance-cash-flow-forecast — Explanation of how cash flow forecasts work.

www.tutor2u.net/business/blog/qa-how-does-the-acid-test-ratio-differ-from-the-current-ratio — Explanation of acid-test and current ratios.

Practice questions

Answer Questions 1–3 using the information below:

Ollie owns a fruit and vegetable market stall. He has been very successful over the past three years and has built up a large and loyal customer base, which has increased each year by 10 per cent. During the pandemic, he noticed that some regular customers were not buying from the stall. He decided he would deliver any leftover stock to these local customers. They were always grateful for the fresh fruit and vegetables.

1. Ollie is thinking about expanding his business. He has decided to enter into a partnership with Jasper. Jasper will focus on the fruit-and-veg delivery service. They need to ensure that they break even in the first year of trading.
   Explain the meaning of the term break-even. [2 marks]

2. Ollie and Jasper need to work out how much it will cost to produce a large box of fruit and veg. They have worked out their costs, which are:
   - Fixed costs: £4000 per year
   - Variable costs: £5 per box
   - Selling price per box: £15 per box

   They sell 100 boxes in their first month. Calculate the sales revenue for the month. [4 marks]

3. Calculate the number of boxes they need to sell in order to break even. [3 marks]

4. State **one** difference between fixed costs and variable costs. [3 marks]

5. Identify **three** ways in which a business can improve its cash flow management. [3 marks]

6. Identify the difference between fixed costs and start-up costs. [2 marks]

7. State **one** example of a fixed cost. [1 mark]

8. State **one** example of a start-up cost. [1 mark]

9. State **one** way in which liabilities and assets are different. [2 marks]

10. State the **two** different types of liabilities. [2 marks]

11. State whether a two-year bank loan would be a current liability, a non-current (long-term) liability, a current asset or a non-current asset. [1 mark]

6 Sources of enterprise funding and business finance

Assignment practice

Your sandwich and panini delivery business has been launched and has proved very popular, and after a year of trading you have decided to expand. You have decided to create a business plan to present to investors who may be interested in supporting your expansion ideas. Several documents have been produced in your first year of trading that you will need to use as part of the financial part of your business plan.

Income statement	
	£
Sales revenue	180,000
Less costs of sales	<u>30,000</u>
	150,000
Less expenses	
Wages and salaries	35,000
Rent	5,000
Operating licence (for business parks)	1,000
Vehicle	5,000
Repairs and maintenance	<u>3,000</u>
	49,000
Net profit	101,000

Cash flow forecast figures:

Opening balance is £10,000
Cash inflows for the 12 months are £6000 (average)
Cash outflows for the 12 months are £3000 (average)

141

NCFE Level 1/2 Technical Award in Business and Enterprise

Statement of financial position

	£	£
Fixed assets		
Premises		50,000
Machinery		1,000
Vehicles		<u>10,000</u>
		61,000
Current assets		
Stock	2,000	
Debtors	1,000	
Prepayment of insurance	1,000	
Cash	<u>3,000</u>	
	7,000	
Current liabilities		
Trade payables	2,000	
Accrual of rates	<u>1,000</u>	
Bank overdraft	3,000	
Working capital		5,000
Long-term liabilities		5,000
Bank overdraft		
Net assets		61,000
Financed by:		
Capital		50,000
Owner's funds		13,000
Less drawings		<u>2,000</u>
		61,000

Tasks:

1. Put together a simple cash flow forecast and explain what the figures from the income statement and statement of financial position show. You could use ratio analysis to show how successful the business has or has not been over the past year. (AO1, AO2, AO3, AO4, AO5)

2. You are considering a number of long-term funding methods for your business. Investigate different methods that you could use in order to expand your business. Remember you have taken on two new members of your team and need a new delivery van. You may need to rent premises in the future, such as a kitchen to keep up with the success of your business. Report all your findings in a document. (AO1, AO2, AO3, AO4)

7 The impact of the external environment on business and enterprise

About this content area

This content area focuses on how a business can be impacted by the external environment. You will learn about:

- The impact of the external environment — How external decisions impact on the business, including taxation, economics, legislation, technology, social aspects such as fashion and trends, the environment and competitors to the business.

7.1 The impact of the external environment

7.1.1 External influences

All businesses are affected by external influences. These are issues that are outside of the business's control. The following would be classed as external influences that affect a business:

- Taxation
- Economics
- Legislation
- Social
- Technological
- Environmental
- The competitive environment.

Taxation

Businesses tend to need to consider three main types of taxation:

- VAT (value added tax) — This is a tax that is added to the goods and services we purchase. There are some exceptions, for example VAT is not added to children's clothes and shoes or to sporting activities. Further information about VAT can be found at: www.gov.uk/guidance/rates-of-vat-on-different-goods-and-services
- Income tax — This is a tax that employees pay from their earnings. The government gives everyone who works a tax-free personal allowance and in order to pay tax employees must earn more than this allowance. In April 2022, this allowance was £12,570 per year. For those who earn less than this amount, no income tax is taken.

- Corporation tax — This is a tax for all businesses that are a limited company. In addition, foreign businesses with a UK office and sports clubs have to pay this tax. A business will be required to keep accurate accounts, prepare a tax return and file the tax return by a specific date so that it knows how much tax it will have to pay.

When there are changes in the taxation rates, businesses need to ensure they apply the correct rates. For example, a change in the VAT rate would mean that the selling price of goods and services either increases or decreases according to the change in the rate. Changes in income tax affect the wages and salaries that are paid to employees. In simple terms, an increase in income tax means that employees receive less money and more money is paid to the government via HMRC. Corporation tax is paid on company profits. If there is an increase in corporation tax rates, then more tax is paid to the government and there is less money to share out and pay to shareholders in the form of dividends.

Activity

1. Find out what the current level of VAT is.
2. A window-cleaning business has to add VAT to the services that it provides to its customers.
   a. If it charges £18 for a basic cleaning service, what would be the VAT amount that it has to add to the overall amount (using the current VAT rate that you researched for question 1)?
   b. If VAT was raised by 2 per cent, what would be the total new price of the service that it charges to its customers?
3. A builder quotes the price of an extension to a property for a customer. It will cost £25,000, but then he has to add VAT.
   a. How much will the VAT cost?
   b. What would the total price of this service be?
   c. If VAT was raised by 2 per cent, what would be the total new price of the extension for the customer?

Economics

Economics can influence and impact on a business in a range of different ways.

Gross domestic product

Gross domestic product (GDP) is a measure of the market value of all of the goods and services produced during a period of time. GDP is a monetary value for either a whole country or a specific region, and the figure is used for international comparisons. It is calculated monthly and reported every three months, which gives a good indication of how a country's economy is performing. A rising GDP demonstrates that more jobs are being created and employees may earn more money. If GDP is falling, it means that the economy is shrinking. If GDP falls twice in a six-month period then this is classed as a recession, which can mean that jobs are lost and pay for employees is frozen as businesses do not have the money to spend.

Key term

Economics How society, which includes governments, businesses and individuals, can manage the production, distribution and consumption of goods and services, and the impact this has on us all.

7 The impact of the external environment on business and enterprise

Interest rates

An interest rate is the cost of borrowing money or the benefit that is gained from saving money.

- Low interest rates encourage customers to buy more goods as there is no benefit in them saving their money. When goods are purchased on credit at low interest rates, for example a mortgage, the repayments are lower, therefore businesses and individuals have more money to spend on other goods and services.
- High interest rates result in customers purchasing fewer goods as their repayments on loans and mortgages are higher. In addition, there is more incentive for them to save money in the bank as they will gain a higher return.

Employment levels

No organisation exists in isolation, therefore a business must take account of the current economic climate. Over time, the economic activity of a country varies, going up and down. It is recognised that the economy usually works in a cycle of decline (downturn or slump), growth, boom and recession. This can be represented in graphical form, as in Figure 7.1.

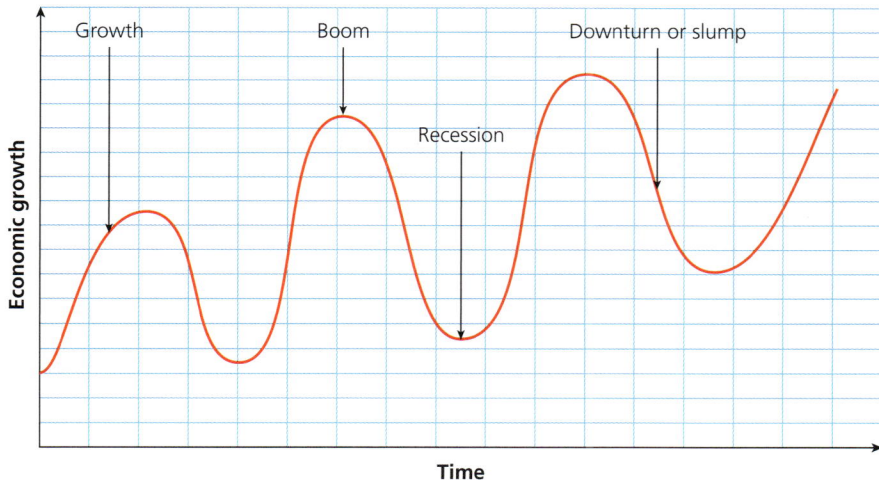

Figure 7.1 The cycle of economic growth and decline

- During a decline period, businesses suffer from a decrease in sales and there is little or no demand for new products or services. The business therefore may not require all the staff that it employs, so it would reduce its workforce. It is unlikely to develop new products during this time.
- During a growth period, customers have more money to spend and are likely to want to purchase new goods or services. Businesses will therefore develop and sell new products, and employment levels will rise as production increases.
- On reaching the boom period, customer spending is at its highest and businesses are likely to introduce and sell a wide range of new products. As before, employment levels will keep rising due to the increases in demand for products and services.

- During a recession, customers have very little money to spend on luxury goods, so businesses need to consider developing cheaper products. The business may reduce its workforce again.

Availability of skills

A business is dependent on the skills that are available in the local area. Organisations based in remote areas often struggle to employ high-quality staff and so employees may need to be brought in from further afield. This can incur extra costs. If specialist staff are required, for example technology experts, there is a strong possibility that employees with these skills may not be available locally. Businesses will need experts who are able to advise and implement appropriate policies to deal with these issues.

Minimum wage

The minimum wage is decided by the government and is the minimum amount of money that businesses must pay their employees. It is stated as an hourly rate. An increase in the minimum wage means that businesses need to pay higher wages. This means costs increase, which reduces profit levels. At the same time, however, individuals will have more money to spend on goods or services as their earnings have increased. This means that sales could potentially increase for businesses.

Legislation

When developing any product, a business must comply with all current legislation. For example, products must comply with up-to-date safety standards. Businesses are also affected by employment law imposed by the government. Employment law aims to protect the rights and responsibilities of employers and employees.

Any new legislation or change to current legislation needs to be considered by all businesses. In many cases, there may be costs involved in making the necessary changes.

Anti-discrimination legislation

Anti-discrimination legislation protects employers and employees and is covered within the Equality Act 2010. This Act includes nine protected characteristics against which it is illegal to discriminate. These are:

- age
- disability
- gender reassignment
- marriage and civil partnership
- pregnancy and maternity
- race
- religion or belief
- sex
- sexual orientation.

Activity

Research the current minimum wage levels using the following website:
www.gov.uk/national-minimum-wage-rates

- How much has the rate increased over the years for under-18s?

7 The impact of the external environment on business and enterprise

Health and safety legislation

Health and safety legislation is concerned with ensuring that employers and employees are kept safe while completing their work. It is everyone's responsibility to keep individuals safe. For example, if a person spills a drink on a floor it can become slippery, so it is the responsibility of the individual to clear up the spillage safely so that others will not slip.

The main piece of legislation covering health and safety is the Health and Safety at Work Act 1974, which states that businesses need to ensure that their employees' health is not affected by the work they complete.

Advertising legislation

Advertising legislation is concerned with businesses adhering to laws to ensure that the goods and services they sell meet the descriptions they state and do what they say that they should. The Trade Descriptions Act 1968 states that accurate descriptions of products/services must be given.

For example, if a business claims that a stain remover for clothes removed all stains including oil, it must be able to do so! If it does not, then the business is claiming something that is untrue in its advertising and therefore is in breach of the Trade Descriptions Act.

The Sale and Supply of Goods Act 1994 focuses on ensuring that businesses produce products that will not harm others, are of satisfactory quality, have nothing wrong with them when purchased, last for a reasonable amount of time, and are suitable for the intended purpose they were purchased for. If any of these are not true when a customer purchases a product, they are within their customer rights to return it to the business, usually with a proof of purchase such as the receipt, so that the business is aware. A business will offer a replacement or a full refund as its reputation can be damaged by any errors in products.

Data protection legislation

Data protection laws exist to ensure that businesses within the UK comply with data privacy. The General Data Protection Regulation Act 2018 (GDPR) came into force to protect individuals. With many of us downloading apps, our personal details are included and it is important that the businesses who own the rights of the app protect our data so that it does not get compromised.

GDPR ensures that:

- personal data must be fairly and lawfully processed and only obtained for specific and legitimate reasons by businesses
- personal data that is kept by a business must be accurate, up to date and not kept for longer than required
- personal data must be kept securely and only specific and relevant information kept.

> **Activity**
>
> In pairs, discuss a product that you or your family have purchased that had a fault. What was the fault, and what did you or your family do? What was the outcome? Share your discussions with the class.

Social

Changes in fashions and trends

Businesses need to adapt to changes in fashions and trends. A business must keep up to date with current wants or it will struggle to survive. One example in recent years is the increased use of reusable products such as water bottles due to environmental concerns. Technological developments are occurring all of the time. Therefore, any new product with electronic components needs to be able to deal with advances in technology.

It is important to remember that technological issues can relate either to the business or to the consumer. For example, most consumers want to purchase the latest up-to-date models; when new mobile phones or tablets are released, there is very little demand for the older models. Businesses need to respond to customers' requirements and ensure they have designed new models, have trained staff so they are able to manufacture and sell the latest technology, and have the machinery available to manufacture the latest models. Businesses may also need to sell off at a much-reduced price any older stock that is out of date and so not appealing to customers.

Technological

Availability of new production equipment

Technological developments occur all the time, so a new product that contains electronic components must be able to deal with advances in technology if it is to remain relevant. For example, the increase in demand for electric cars has made car manufacturers consider how these can be produced in a more efficient way to meet the rising demand. Technological advances of new production equipment therefore have to be implemented into the production process of electric cars.

It is important to remember that technological issues may relate to either the business's products or to prospective consumers. For example, consumers often want to purchase the most up-to-date versions of a product. This is especially true where mobile phones or tablets are concerned as there is very little demand for the previous models.

Increase and improvement in mobile technology

Businesses need to ensure their products incorporate all the latest features expected by the customer — carrying out customer research and then developing new features to meet these needs is likely to be costly. A business may need to invest in new machinery or factories to produce the new models as well as invest in training staff to manufacture and sell the new models.

> **Activity**
>
> If you were to upgrade your current mobile phone, what features would you expect on your upgrade? Compare your answers with another person in the class.

7 The impact of the external environment on business and enterprise

Growth of e-commerce

E-commerce is the buying and selling of goods and services online. Many businesses have an online presence, meaning that customers can purchase items from them on websites. When the pandemic occurred in the UK in 2020, the government instructed shops to close. At the time, businesses were not aware of the likely impact of this on their livelihood and quickly had to adjust their trading methods if they were to survive.

Digital sales were already increasing, with businesses like Amazon and online auction sites such as eBay becoming ever more popular. During the pandemic this increased, with customers wanting to continue to be able to purchase items to be delivered directly to their houses. This worked well for many larger businesses, but was a struggle for smaller business as they had to diversify their operations. For example, many restaurants offered a takeaway service, with meals ordered online and collected or delivered directly to the customers. Other restaurants offered a 'cook-at-home' option, where they supplied the ingredients to cook a dish or provided a ready-to-cook option. Some businesses continued to offer these services after restrictions were eased. Business have continued to see the importance of e-commerce and to embrace this method of doing business.

Environmental

Businesses need to consider the impact of their operations on the environment. With the world being more affected by climate change, businesses will want to be environmentally friendly as we are now more aware of the damage that we are doing to our planet. The UK government has imposed legal constraints to force businesses to:

- cut down on energy consumption
- reduce waste
- reduce pollution
- reduce carbon emissions
- dispose of waste responsibly.

Figure 7.2 Many plastics end up in our rivers and oceans

Businesses also face pressure from consumers to strive towards sustainability. One example of a successful government initiative was introducing a charge for single-use carrier bags. According to the government, since the introduction of the charge in 2015, single-use plastic bag usage in major supermarkets has dropped by 86 per cent.

Source: https://commonslibrary.parliament.uk/research-briefings/cbp-7241

The competitive environment

Number of competitors

Understanding its direct competitors will help to reduce the challenges and risks a business may face. Competitor analysis is an important aspect of business research as it enables the business to identify its main competitors: the businesses that are producing or selling similar products/services. Once these are identified, the business can then investigate them further.

Any business wants to ensure that customers purchase its products/services rather than those of its competitors. This can only be achieved if the business has information about these identified competitors so that it can persuade customers to purchase what the business is offering instead.

An easy way for a business to compare its product/service with similar ones is to make a competitor chart. Look at the example in Table 7.1 for a business that is going to produce a new healthy snack bar in this competitive sector.

Table 7.1 Competition chart for a business that is going to produce a new healthy snack bar

Product	Age of customers	Men/women/children	Price	Where purchased
Humzinger	2–6 years	Children	£1.50 for five	Supermarkets
Special K Red Berries bar	Adults 18+	Women	£1.99 for five	Supermarkets
Nature Valley Canadian Maple Syrup bar	Adults 18+	Men/women	£2.40 for five	Supermarkets
Cadbury Brunch Bar	10 years+	Men/women/children	£1.99 for six	Supermarkets

Looking at the results, you can see that the products are sold in boxes of five or six bars, and all of them are available in supermarkets, where there are several competing products on the shelves. This information may make a business consider whether or not it wants to enter into this market.

Growth opportunities

A business will want to seek new methods to continue to grow its business operations and to remain competitive in an ever-changing business world. Businesses cannot remain complacent; they have to keep ahead otherwise they will get left behind. The pandemic demonstrated the ability of many businesses to adapt their business strategies to continue to operate within the government-imposed lockdowns so that they could continue to trade. This did not work for all businesses, but for many these different ways of trading have continued and even changed the way that they operate today. For example, restaurants had to close their doors but instead were able to offer a takeaway or home delivery service to their loyal customers. Many have continued this and still operate with table service, takeaway services and home delivery!

Businesses that did not already trade online quickly learnt the importance of having a website to sell products and so created one. Some businesses such as small independent shops had to physically close the doors on their business premises, but moved to successfully trade online and have seen this as a good and positive business move.

7 The impact of the external environment on business and enterprise

If a business is selling a product that has universal appeal but has yet to target a full range of customers, it could decide to sell its product in new markets. For more on entering new markets, see Section 2.3.5.

Benefits:

- If a business can successfully tap into a new market, it may see its sales — and therefore its profits — increase considerably.
- There is the possibility that by exploring new markets, the benefits gained will balance out the risks of current investment.
- By exploring new markets, an alternative is available when an existing market starts to decline.

Disadvantages:

- This strategy may not be suitable for all products. Certain products may only be popular in certain geographic locations, for example kilts may be popular in Scotland but will have a limited market in Wales.
- Exploration into new markets may require staff to have new skills — this could be expensive and increase costs.

> **Remember**
>
> - There are three different forms of taxation: VAT; income tax; corporation tax.
> - Any new legislation or change to current legislation needs to be considered by all businesses. In many cases, there may be costs involved in making necessary changes.
> - The external influence of economics can impact on a business in a range of ways, for example tax, economics, legislation, social, technological, environment, competitive.
> - A business will want to seek new methods to continue to grow its operations and to remain competitive in an ever-changing business world.
> - Technological developments occur all the time and it is important that businesses are informed and react to these changes to remain competitive.
> - Businesses need to consider the impact of their operations on the environment, with the UK government imposing legal constraints to force businesses to cut down on energy consumption, reduce waste, reduce pollution, reduce carbon emissions and dispose of waste responsibly.

Test yourself

1. Define external influences on a business.
2. Identify two different forms of external influence on a business.
3. What does VAT stand for?
4. How can new legislation impact on a business?
5. Describe e-commerce.

Practice questions

1. Identify **three** different forms of external influences that can impact on a business and its stakeholders. [3 marks]
2. Explain how an understanding of social trends can help a business. [3 marks]
3. Explain how the UK government has encouraged businesses to consider the environment in their operations. Give an example to illustrate this. [4 marks]
4. GDP is a measurement that is used internationally to measure the economic performance of a country. Analyse how useful it can be and its implications for business. [9 marks]

Read about it

Sawyer, M. *The UK Economy: A manual of applied economics* (OUP, 2005) — Fundamental information about the UK economy.

Sloman, J. and Sutcliffe, M. *Economics for Business* (Financial Times/Prentice Hall, 2004) — Details on key economics topics relating to business.

Taylor, M. and Mankiw, N. *Economics* (Cengage Learning, 2020) — An overview of microeconomics and macroeconomics.

www.peterjones.com — Information about Peter Jones as an entrepreneur, including short videos.

www.bbc.co.uk/news/business — Up-to-date news articles relating to business and the current economic climate.

www.gov.uk/browse/tax — Up-to-date information from the UK government, including key taxation details.

Assignment practice

Since you started your sandwich and panini delivery buisness, a major issue has been the increases in costs to the business due to dramatic increases in the costs of food, electricity and gas. Added to this, the government has increased taxes as well as forcing businesses to consider the environmental aspects of their operations. You have now gone into a partnership with an old school friend and asked her to investigate the impact of these changes for your business.

You have asked for a report on the external environment influences and how your business can better plan for this in the future.

Tasks:

1. Create a report that explains how external environment influences will affect the business and what the business will have to do to cover these potential costs. (AO1, AO2, AO3)
2. Analyse the implications for the customers and profits of the business. (AO1, AO2, AO3)

8 Business and enterprise planning

About this content area

This content area focuses on how a business and enterprise activity can plan for the future. You will learn about:

- The purposes and benefits of planning — The benefits to the business of planning, both in the short term and long term.
- The sections of a business plan — The various areas that are included within a business plan: an executive summary; research required; market analysis; marketing, people and operations; the financial plan.

8.1 Business and enterprise planning

8.1.1 Purposes and benefits of planning

Planning is an important aspect in all areas of life. If you want to do anything, then a certain amount of time will need to be spent making the plans before they are put into action.

Business planning is an essential tool in order to successfully start or maintain the running of a business. At first it can be complex as well as time consuming, but with careful planning, the process does get easier.

Purpose of business planning

All businesses have to plan for the future. If an organisation does not keep up with changes, it may end up closing. This has been the case for several large businesses in the past few years. Planning how a business operates is crucial for its continued success.

The purpose of planning involves five main areas: informing potential investors; informing existing investors and employees; monitoring progress; identifying necessary resources; reducing risks.

Informing potential investors

Potential investors are individuals who take an interest in a business and may look to provide financial support. They could be private individuals, businesses or banks that loan money to the business. In order for this to occur, investors will want to know the plans for the business and

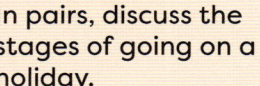

Activity

In pairs, discuss the stages of going on a holiday.
- What do you need to think about before you get in the car or on the train, coach or aeroplane to go to your chosen destination and enjoy your time away? Write a list of what needs to happen.
- Share your list with your class.

how their support will be used so that they can be reassured that their investments will be used sensibly to allow the business to thrive and grow.

Funding and finance is one of the key elements of planning for any business, as without this an organisation will not be able to determine how much finance is required to start and keep running successfully. Section 6.1.1 detailed the range of different funding methods, some of which will be more appropriate for one business than another. When providing finance for any organisation, lenders need to be convinced that the money will be repaid, and therefore it is important that they can see how capable the business will be in paying the money back. This can be achieved by:

- having a realistic plan for the business
- providing assets, such as a house, to secure any loans
- using the owner's money as part of the funding for the business
- understanding how cash will flow in and out of the business
- identifying potential sales and profits to be made
- having evidence of completed market research
- providing and demonstrating the determination, skills and communication required to make the business a success.

These different aspects will be detailed in a business plan (see Section 8.1.2). Investors will want to see this document before providing any form of finance to a business.

Informing employees

The future plans for the business will be shared by management with employees. It is important for staff to be aware of the different plans for and directions of the business as it could have implications for their roles.

Planning enables a business to review its current position and whether changes are realistic or necessary, and then to decide the process. Operational planning involves all functional areas, as any changes will have a knock-on effect on other areas.

For example, a garden furniture business is looking to expand its staff in preparation for a busy spring and summer. It needs a designer and production and sales staff. The Human Resources function within the business is important for the planning stages. Forecasting the staff required for a business to fulfil its objectives is hard, but without staff input, customer orders might not be fulfilled, which would have a negative impact on the business. Once decisions have been made about staff numbers, the manager needs to make several decisions to ensure the plans can be fulfilled. These decisions include:

- the number of new staff required
- what types of contracts are required
- the job roles
- the training period, especially if specialist equipment will be used by these new job roles
- the wage/salary for each individual.

8 Business and enterprise planning

Some individuals who have worked for the business for a period of time may have the opportunity to apply for promotions within the company. If this is the case, they will need training in their new roles. Any form of training takes time and the role will not be being completed fully while the training is taking place; the business will need to be aware of and make arrangements for this. This could mean the individual who completed the role in the past continues during the time of training and then hands over the responsibility once the new person has successfully completed all their training.

Monitoring progress

Monitoring a business's progress is the role of its owners or managers and this can only happen with proper planning. Unless plans are made, it is very hard to know whether a business is performing to its expected levels. Initially, setting the company's aims and objectives gives the organisation focus. Aims and objectives will change throughout the life of a business, but initially these may be quite simple, such as to survive the first 12 months of trade. Specific objectives give a business clear direction. Objectives should be SMART:

- **S**pecific — State what should be achieved.
- **M**easurable — Have a measuring tool to decide if the objectives have been achieved.
- **A**greed — Have aims and objectives that everyone involved understands and agrees to.
- **R**ealistic — Be achievable in terms of the competition and market.
- **T**ime-bound — Be monitored by a timeframe, which should be achievable.

Ensuring that objectives are SMART and that aims can be met makes it easier for the business to make plans. Examples of aims and objectives could be:

- Achieving specific sales targets.
- Increasing market share.
- Reaching a production target.
- Making a specific amount of profit.
- Breaking even in the first year.

Identifying necessary resources

We have already established that it is important to plan the future of a business. If the plan involves expanding the business operation, bigger premises may be required. The organisation would need to consider if it can afford this by reviewing its finances. Bigger premises would mean an increase in bills for the new building, such as for electricity, gas and insurance. The business might also need new staff. This clearly demonstrates that any operational change can impact dramatically on the business, so it is important that change is planned so that the required resources can be sourced in time for the planned changes.

Reducing risks

Risks are things that could harm a business, so it is important that it plans to reduce any risks. If a situation does occur that could pose a risk to the business, a planned process should have been devised so that individuals know what to do.

For example, a risk that could occur is staff illness, as this can have an immediate impact on the operation of a business. Power failures can also impact on operations, particularly for businesses that are reliant on technology — which most are these days for communication alone! A business would need to provide extra training to cover particular roles if sickness occurs or to purchase and provide backup generators in case of power failure. Natural disasters such as flooding or fire can be disastrous for an organisation. For example, if a business knows that it is positioned near a flood plain, then suitable planning should be made in case flooding occurs. If stock is stored in that location, an alternative storage location in a different area could be sought. Having such plans in place means that even if the business is flooded, the stock is safe.

An organisation could ask itself certain questions:

1. When, why, where and how might the identified risks occur?
2. Are the risks internal to the business? (Internal risks such as staff sickness can be managed by the organisation.)
3. Are the potential problems external to the business? (External problems include changes to the taxes it has to pay.)
4. Who might need to take control of the problem?
5. Who might be affected by the issue?

A business could also consider a variety of different 'What if ...' scenarios, which is when the organisation focuses on what it would do if something happened. For example, 'What if there was no access to the internet?' or 'What if our suppliers suddenly went out of business?'

Businesses could also think about the worst-case scenario. This might seem a little dramatic, but it makes the organisation focus on what to do if such a crisis should unfortunately occur. This will help it deal better with smaller problems and hopefully keep positive!

Certain situations may not be able to be planned for, for example the Covid-19 pandemic. Businesses were not prepared for lockdowns and the restrictions that were imposed on all our lives, and the pandemic had major implications for the business world. While many businesses successfully adapted, others did not and unfortunately did not survive.

A business may decide to ask for advice and support from other organisations. Some local authorities offer external support in the form of mentoring, where a business is put in contact with an established business individual who can provide it with help and support. Mentors could provide help with areas such as market trends, competition and research. They may offer a different viewpoint on the research an individual has produced or identify errors that have occurred. They will not complete specific work but will point the business in the right direction so

8 Business and enterprise planning

it can complete the necessary work. The business may retain the mentor for several months or until it feels confident to operate fully on its own. Having a mentor enables an organisation to seek advice and support.

Benefits of planning

The benefit of having a clear vision for a business is that the people involved can plan for the future. If issues occur, staff will know that these have been thought through and contingency plans have been made, so that the business can continue to be successful.

Sadly, this was not the case for some organisations that have ceased to trade. This was often because they had not kept up with changes in the markets. For example, Toys 'R' Us was reliant on customers going to its large shops, which were often in out-of-town retail parks. With the increase in internet sales and with rival businesses offering cheaper deals on goods, sales at Toys 'R' Us started to fall and it appeared not to be able to compete. The business had to maintain the high rents and bills for the retail shops, compared to internet companies that just have to have suitable warehouses with staff to store the stock and the ability to deliver the products to customers. Overall this is cheaper, which is why lower prices and special offers can be given to customers. By contrast, Toys 'R' Us had to charge more. It had not seen how the increase in internet sales could impact on its business and did not plan effectively, resulting in it ceasing to trade in 2018.

There are five main benefits from planning for businesses:

- Identifying short- and long-term finance needs.
- Helping in raising finance.
- Reducing the likelihood of cash flow problems.
- Aligning employees' focus with that of the business.
- Ensuring resources are available when needed.

Activity

Oxfordshire Local Enterprise Partnership (OxLEP) is an organisation that offers a range of advice and guidance to create a dynamic, sustainable and growing economy in the Oxfordshire area: www.oxfordshirelep.com

The Growth Hub is another service that offers similar support to businesses in the south-west of the country: www.heartofswgrowthhub.co.uk

- Research both organisations to discover what they can offer businesses.
- Report your findings back to the rest of your class.

Identifying short- and long-term finance needs, and helping in raising finance

Having a good business plan will enable an organisation to identify the short- and long-term finance needs that it may have in order to implement its plans. See Section 6.1.1 for information related to funding types.

Reducing likelihood of cash flow problems

By planning for the future, the business will focus on ensuring that its finances remain positive, to enable it to pay bills and balance the inflows and outflows of the business. This is important as it reduces the risk of cash flow problems for the business. Keeping accurate records, knowing when payments have to be made, and customers paying the business on time are all important aspects of having a good understanding of financial management. We established in Section 6.2 the importance of financial documents, such as break-even, cash flow forecasts, income statements, statements of financial position and ratio analysis. All of these form the financial strategy for the business. Ratio analysis provides data that shows how the organisation is performing. Having all this information together means that if, for example, the business wants to expand its operation, it can see whether this is a realistic option and the timeframe in which this could occur.

Aligning employees' focus with that of the business

Sharing the plans for the business will affect the employees who work for the organisation. If the business is upfront and honest about the plans, this will benefit the business and the employees in the long term. It could be that a need for additional staff has been identified, which means planning the process to recruit these new employees. Another benefit could be that promotional opportunities could occur for employees who want to progress their career due to the changes within the business. If the business was to relocate to larger premises, extensive planning would be needed. If employees are not happy with the plans they might leave, which would leave the business with a range of other issues. Keeping employees informed will mean that they are reassured of their position within the business, how their job or working conditions will be affected and the duration of the changes.

Ensuring resources are available when needed

Planning for changes within a business means it can identify the extra resources that are needed and ensure that they are there when needed. The types of resources that may be needed could be specific machinery or equipment, vehicles for deliveries or even new staff to complete the tasks required in order to run the business. For example, if a business has its busiest trading period in the summer, it may choose to employ seasonal workers for just the summer season. Many coastal businesses in the UK operate in this way as they know that the school summer holidays will be popular with visitors to the local area. They therefore want to ensure that they can gain maximum sales during the period from June to September each year.

Test yourself

1. Why would an investor want to know the future plans for a specific business?
2. Why is it important for a business to plan for potential risks?
3. If a business has cash flow problems, how can this affect it?

Activity

Jamie has a first aid business called First Plus, which attends local events and provides first aid cover in case it is required. It attends small village fetes, local food festivals and sports events in the locality. During the pandemic, no business was generated as all events were cancelled. This gave Jamie the time to think about how to relaunch his business once restrictions were lifted. He decided to attend larger events, but he needs some help with planning this and has asked for your help regarding the purpose and benefits of planning for his relaunched business venture.

- Compose an email to Jamie outlining the purpose and benefits of planning for the relaunched First Plus business.

8 Business and enterprise planning

8.1.2 Sections of a business plan

A **business plan** is a formal document that details how the organisation will operate and succeed. The document will be read by potential investors, so it is important it is clear and ensures the reader is fully aware of all aspects of the business. It should answer all of the questions that the reader has prior to reading the plan.

A business plan will include several different sections in a particular order:

- Executive summary
- Primary and secondary research
- Market analysis
- Marketing
- People and operations
- Financial plan

We will look at each part in detail.

Key term

Business plan A plan aimed at investors such as banks, which may invest money into a business.

Executive summary

The **executive summary** introduces the business and details:

- the company name
- the product or service provided, in the form of a summary of the business
- the reasons for the product or service
- the target market
- the legal structure
- the finance required.

The executive summary also details the aims and objectives and the structure of the business and its legal status. This first section is important, as the reader will use it to decide if they want to find out more about the organisation. If the business idea does not interest the potential investor, they may not continue to the next section.

Key term

Executive summary Introduces the business and details its name, the product or service it provides, its target market and legal structure, and the finance required.

Primary and secondary research

The next section of a business plan is based on a market analysis of the business's products/services. It is a chance for the organisation to describe the competition that the product will be up against, in terms of:

- Target market — The business's main target market, which is the people or companies the products/services are aimed at, where they are located, their characteristics and the number of customers it wishes to attract.
- Labour needs — The business will need to plan for the employees that will be required in order to satisfy the demand for and supply of the products/services once they are advertised and produced. It is important it knows the specific skills that will be required from potential new employees. For example, if it needs employees with an understanding of finance, it may also want these individuals to be able

to complete all elements required within a finance role. A business will also want to plan for the costs of new staff.
- Premises needs — As a business grows, so may the premises that it operates within. Some businesses start off at the home of the owner of the business and, with success, they have to find new premises to operate from. This will involve researching different locations, considering the facilities required and how big the premises should be to accommodate the business. They will need to budget and work out what the business can afford. The bigger the premises, the more costs will increase, such as heating, lighting and rent, which all need to be considered by the business. A business plan will document all these predictions.
- Equipment — as with premises, the growing success of a business will mean that the equipment required could change over time. A business plan will enable a business to detail the items needed, the reasons why and the costs that will be incurred.
- Raw materials and/or components — A business that produces products and services will require a range of different raw materials and/or components to make the required items. At certain times of the year a business may require more of these, so the business will need to plan for this in terms of the quantity needed, the costs and who will supply the items that are needed.

Market analysis

The next section within the business plan focuses on the market analysis, which specifically focuses on the target market(s), how the business can compete in the chosen market(s) in terms of competitive environment (the predicted growth of the market), and the potential suppliers that the business may use and why they have been selected. It is important to focus on these areas so that potential investors can trust that the research that has been completed is thorough.

Marketing

This section details the marketing of the business using the 4 Ps — product, price, place and promotion. (For more on the 4 Ps, see Section 2.3.) This part of the business plan will detail what the USP is for each of the products/services. It contains information regarding market research that has been completed, and the distribution channels that will be used so that the customers or suppliers get the products/services they have ordered. This section also has details of the different promotional methods that will be used. This may include examples of promotional materials, as well as figures relating to the overall costs of producing the products compared to the selling prices.

People and operations

The next section of the business plan is based on the people involved and the operations of the business. It describes how the organisation is structured and managed, with a focus on two main areas:

- People considerations — This involves focusing on a breakdown of the number of employees required to run the business. A business must plan the structure that it wants for the business to help plan the staff required to successfully run the operation. This part of the plan details the different managers and how many staff they are responsible for, so that investors can get an overall understanding of how the business will be structured. Knowing this will ensure that the business can focus on the skills and training needs of staff and the costs involved.
- Operational considerations — This section has information about the production processes that will make the products/services, as well as the equipment and material requirements. It also includes the business's quality control procedures, the distribution methods of the products and services to its customers and the overall costs of these different elements of the business operation.

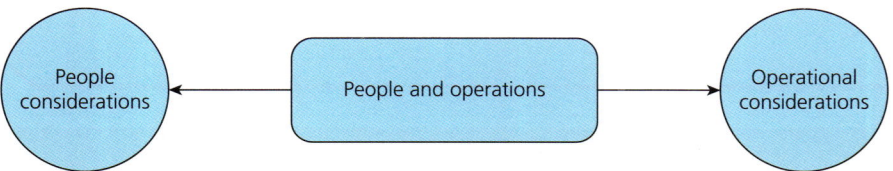

Figure 8.1 People and operational considerations

Financial plan

The final section of a business plan is the financial plan. This part of the document details the required start-up costs and the running costs (fixed and variable costs) of the business, as well as the cash flow forecast, break-even charts, calculations and analysis. It also contains information regarding the income statement, which will include the gross and net profit figures and the forecast statement of financial position, as well as any plans for growth and development in the future. Having six sections to a business plan enables a variety of investors to focus on different elements. An investor could be a business with different specialists within the firm; the marketing director would have more specific knowledge for the marketing section than the finance director, who would be more interested in the financial plan section.

Test yourself

1. Why do businesses produce a business plan?
2. Identify the six different sections within a business plan and write a sentence to describe each section.

Activity

Write an article that details why it is important to complete a business plan if you want to gain finance from any form of financial institution. Give examples where you can.

Activity

Use the internet to research and download a business plan template. Working in small groups, decide on a business idea that you would like to develop. Complete the business plan template for your business idea.

NCFE Level 1/2 Technical Award in Business and Enterprise

Remember

- Business planning is an essential tool in order to successfully start or maintain the running of a business.
- Business planning demonstrates the business's vision and details how it will achieve this vision.
- The benefit of having a clear vision for a business is that the people involved can plan for the future.
- Business planning enables an organisation to plan for a variety of situations that may occur, which could be internal or external to the business.
- Risks to a business can be planned for, which reduces the overall risk.
- A business plan will be read by potential investors who may want to invest in the business.
- Potential investors are individuals who take an interest in a business and provide financial support and will be interested in the future plans of a business.
- A business plan can monitor the progress of the business in terms of performance.
- There are six different sections to a business plan: executive summary; primary and secondary research; market analysis; marketing; people and operations; financial plan.

Practice questions

1. Identify three different purposes of planning for a business. [3 marks]
2. A business plan is an important document. Who will be most interested in the details of a business plan? [1 mark]
3. Look at the following image of a naturally occurring problem that could affect a business.

Figure 8.2 A sinkhole

   Sinkholes in the UK seem to be reported more frequently and can occur after heavy rainfall. Advise an organisation how it should plan for such a situation, which could affect all aspects of its business. [4 marks]
4. How can planning reduce cash flow problems? Explain your answer. [4 marks]
5. If an employee is not happy with future planning for the business, what may they do? [1 mark]
6. What are the different elements of a financial plan that will be included in a business plan? [7 marks]
7. Why is primary and secondary research an important element of a business plan? Explain your answer, giving examples. [4 marks]

8 Business and enterprise planning

Read about it

www.natwest.com/business/running-your-business/writing-a-business-plan.html — NatWest bank tips for business planning.

www.businessballs.com/strategy-innovation/business-planning-andmarketing-strategy — Tips on preparing a business plan and marketing strategy.

www.heartofswgrowthhub.co.uk — Advice on how to start and grow a business.

www.princes-trust.org.uk/help-for-young-people/tools-resources/business-tools/business-plans — Advice from the Prince's Trust on writing a business plan.

www.princes-trust.org.uk/help-for-young-people/tools-resources/business-tools — Further business advice from the Prince's Trust.

Assignment practice

You have completed a range of tasks based on your successful sandwich and panini delivery service to companies based in business parks on the outskirts of your town. You have sucessfully established the business and now are looking to expand. For this you need to apply for a loan. You will need to create a business plan using all the information that you have gathered from the other tasks that you have completed as part of the practice NEA. It is important that you follow the format below:

- Executive summary
- Primary and secondary research
- Market analysis
- Marketing
- People and operations
- Financial plan

Tasks:

1 Write a description of your business and how successful it has been in the first year of trading. Provide some details of what your business supplies to customers. (AO1, AO2)

2 Why does delivering to business parks work? You now know that there is demand for this service on other business parks, but how do you know this? What are your plans for expansion? Explain all this and more in the market analysis section of your business plan. (AO2, AO3, AO4)

3 Provide some examples of the marketing that you intend to do if your business loan is granted, and provide some costs for this. Customers currently order on an app, but could there be other methods that you might want to think about? (AO1, AO2, AO3)

4 You previously went into a partnership with an old friend due to expansion and took on two new members of staff. However, you have recognised that you will need even more staff to help you manage the expanded business so two more people will be required.

You have also decided to introduce a team leader role, which could be a promotion for a member of staff. This individual will be in charge of training new staff, monitoring their performance and ordering the stock required each week. In the people and operations section of your business plan, describe how many new staff are needed and why, as well as what tasks they will complete as part of their jobs. Will you be in charge? (AO1, AO2, AO3, AO4)

5 The final part of the business plan is the financial aspects. You need to put together a cash flow forecast as well as explaining what the figures from the income statement and statement of financial position show. You could use ratio analysis to show how successful the business has or has not been over the past year. Your completed business plan should be handed to your teacher on or before the given deadline date. (AO1, AO2, AO3, AO4, AO5)

GLOSSARY

Aim The goals that a business intends to achieve.

Annual General Meeting A meeting that happens each year for shareholders and details how the business has performed and the future plans for the business.

Annual percentage rate (APR) The amount charged in interest to a customer who has taken out a loan.

Articles of Association The written rules of running the business, which are agreed by the shareholders and directors.

Assets Resources that a business owns so that it can operate.

Attributes Qualities that individuals naturally possess, which make them individual.

Brand How a business is identified by others, such as consumers and competitors.

Break-even The level of output at which total costs equal total revenue. This is the point at which a business makes no profit and no loss.

Business plan A plan aimed at investors such as banks, which may invest money into a business.

Carbon footprint The amount of carbon dioxide released into the atmosphere as a result of the activities of a business.

Cash flow Shows a business if it will have enough cash in the future to keep running the company, as well as ensuring that the business owners plan for the future.

Cash inflow Money that is coming into the business.

Cash outflow Money that is going out of the business.

Census A survey conducted by the government every ten years to determine key information about the population.

Chain of command The line of communication and authority within a business.

Closing balance The amount of cash a business has at the end of the year.

Competitive pricing Setting a price that is similar to that of competitors.

Contract of employment A formal document, which both the employee and employer sign, agreeing to the terms and conditions.

Cost of sales The costs to a business from making products or services, such as materials.

Costs Financial costs that have to be paid in order for a business to function.

Crowdfunding When many different people give money, often for the purpose of starting a new project.

Current assets Items that the business has that are cash or near-cash, such as stock, money owed to it and cash that is in the bank.

Current liabilities Short-term debts the business has that will need to be paid back within a year.

Customer profile Researching vital information about customers to ensure that products and services appeal to them.

Delegation Allocating specific tasks to team members to complete by a given deadline.

Demand Supplying customers with the products and services that they want within the required timeframe.

Dividend A share of the company's profits.

Economics How society, which includes governments, businesses and individuals, can manage the production, distribution and consumption of goods and services, and the impact this has on us all.

Entrepreneur A risk-taker who sets up a business or businesses with the aim of making large amounts of profit.

Equilibrium price The price that a business should charge for its product.

Glossary

Executive summary Introduces the business and details its name, the product or service it provides, its target market and legal structure, and the finance required.

Expenses The costs that the business incurs on a day-to-day basis while operating.

External growth Business growth by buying or taking over other businesses.

External recruitment When a business recruits and employs a new person to the business who has the skills, knowledge and experience required for the job role.

External training When employees go to a location outside of the office and receive training from external trainers.

Fixed costs Costs that do not change no matter how many products are produced, for example rent, loans, advertising and salaries, etc.

Focus group A group of customers that comes together to talk about their experiences, thoughts and opinions.

Franchise A business where the franchisor (the owner of the business idea) grants a licence (the franchise) to another business (the franchisee) to operate its brand or business idea.

Funding A method of gaining finance for a business.

Gross profit The difference between the money a business received from selling goods and services and the cost of making the products or services. It is calculated by subtracting the sales revenue figure from the cost of sales.

Induction training Training that gives new employees specific information about the business and how to complete their job role.

Innovation A new idea or method, or the process of using new ideas and methods.

Interest An amount of money that is added on to a loan and must be repaid by the customer.

Internal growth How a business has grown from where it originally started to the current time and where it strives to be in the future.

Internal recruitment When a business seeks to fill a vacant position from within the business so an existing employee gains a new role within the same business — often a promotion.

Internal training When employees receive training at the business location, from trainers who are either from within the business or come into the business.

Liabilities Debts that a business may have incurred while trading.

Limited liability When the business owners are liable only up to the amount of money they have invested in the business.

Loan A method of gaining finance from a financial institution. The loan must be repaid with interest within an agreed amount of time.

Loss Occurs when the total costs that the business has to pay are more than the revenue that the business earns from selling its products and services.

Margin of safety A business will determine the amount sales that need to be made before the break even point is achieved which means that they are within the tolerated levels. This will mean that the business will not make a profit but also not make a loss.

Market A place where buyers and sellers come together to trade goods and services.

Market research The actions that a business will use to gather information about customers' needs and wants.

Marketing mix The 4 Ps of marketing, i.e. product, price, place and promotion.

Market-orientated business A business that produces goods based on customer wants and needs.

Mass market A large, wide ranging market, usually with high sales and many competitors.

Memorandum of Association A legal document that is signed by initial shareholders agreeing to form the business.

Merger A form of external growth for two businesses that voluntarily decide to become one organisation.

Mission statement A formal document that states the business's vision for what it is striving to achieve.

Motivator Something that provides a reason for an entrepreneur to be successful.

Net cash flow The total inflow received minus the cash outflows.

Glossary

Net profit A more accurate calculation of how the business is doing than gross profit, as it takes into account the costs that the business incurs. It is calculated by subtracting all expenses from the gross profit figure.

Niche market A small, specialist market, usually with low sales and fewer competitors.

Non-current (fixed) assets Show the value of significant purchases that a business has that help run the business, such as machinery, technology or transport.

Non-current liabilities Long-term debts that the business will have, such as a loan for machinery that helps the business with efficiency, which will take longer than a year to pay back.

Objective A precise and measurable step to complete a business's goals.

Opening balance The amount of cash a business has at the start of the year.

Partnership A business that is owned and controlled by two or more individuals.

Patent A licence that gives the holder the exclusive right for a set time to produce and sell the patented product and to exclude others from making, using or selling the invention.

Place How the product or service is distributed to consumers.

Price How the product or service is priced to make a profit.

Penetration pricing Introducing a product at a lower price than competitors to attract customers, then gradually increasing the price over time.

Price skimming Introducing a product at a high price, then gradually lowering the price over time.

Primary research When a business completes original research that it needs for a specific purpose.

Product How the product or service is designed or invented to make it something that consumers will want to buy.

Product development The processes of bringing a product from being a concept through to reaching the market.

Product life cycle Traces the journey of a product from its development and launch to its removal from sale to the public.

Product-orientated business A business that produces only goods that it is good at making.

Profit The business owner's reward for investing in the business organisation.

Profit maximisers When the main aim of a business is to make profit.

Promotion How consumers are informed about the product or service and persuaded to buy it.

Qualitative data Information that provides a business with an in-depth understanding of key issues, which can help when developing business ideas.

Quantitative data Information that is useful for statistical analysis and review to aid business decisions.

Ratios Calculations that enable a business to judge how it is performing.

Revenue The money that a business makes from selling its products/services.

Sales revenue The amount of money that a business receives from selling goods and services. It is calculated by multiplying the quantity of items sold by the selling price.

Secondary research Gathering data and information that has been collected before.

Share (owners') capital When a company raises money by selling shares in the business, which gives the buyers a part-ownership of the business.

Skills The ability of an individual to do a task well.

Sole trader A business that is owned and controlled by one person.

Span of control The number of people each manager is responsible for.

Stages of recruitment The different processes that a business goes through to ensure it employs the right person for an advertised job role, such as devising a job advert, creating a job description, etc.

Supply Knowing the amount of a good or service that is available to businesses or customers and providing this service.

Takeover When a business acquires control of another organisation.

Target customer A group of customers with similar tastes at which a business enterprise aims its products.

Glossary

Target market A particular group of customers at which a product or service is aimed.

Trend A popular product in fashion at a specific time.

Unlimited liability When the business owners are personally liable for the debts of the business in the event that the business cannot pay them.

Variable costs Costs that vary directly with the level of output, for example stock, raw materials and packaging costs.

Wholesaler A business that sells goods in large quantities to retailers at low prices.

INDEX

acid-test ratio 137
adding value 65
advertising 43, 44, 50–2, 57–8, 65
    legislation 147
aims 9–15, 24, 25, 27, 155
annual percentage rate (APR) 114
appraisals 85
assets 123, 133, 136, 137, 138
attributes of entrepreneurs 6–7
banks 26, 113, 114, 135, 138, 153
Boston Matrix 69
brand image 43, 61, 70–1
brand loyalty 71–2
break-even 118–20, 124–8, 161
business angels 115
business growth 105–9, 150–1
    challenges of 110
business plans 159–61
capital 133
carbon footprint 13
cash cows 69
cash flow forecast 128–30, 137–8
    problems 138–9, 157–8
cell production 98–9
communication 5, 76, 109
community 4, 10, 25, 26, 27
competition 31–2, 38, 67, 149–50
    chart 150
competitive pricing 47
contracts of employment 79, 81–2
cost of sales 131
costs 121–2
    fixed 118, 120, 121–2, 124, 125, 126
    reducing 12, 22
    start-up 121, 161
    total 120, 124, 125, 126
    variable 118, 120, 122, 124, 126
Covid-19 pandemic 32, 107, 115, 124, 149, 150, 156
crowdfunding 115–16
current ratio 136–7
customer(s) 25, 26, 34
    -led approach 42
    loyalty 71–2
    profiling 56, 61, 66, 71
    service 101–3
    target 29–31
data protection 35, 57, 147
data types 39–40
debtors 123, 138
decision-making 7, 22, 34
delayering 22
delegation 22, 109

demand 32, 44, 65
desk market research 38–40
disciplinary action 87
discrimination 14, 146
diseconomies of scale 109
distribution channels 48
diversification 66, 67, 149
diversity 14
dividends 116
e-commerce 48, 49, 149
economic cycle 145–6
economics 144–6
economies of scale 41, 108–9
emails 57
employee(s)
    appraisals 85
    cash flow problems 138
    contract 79, 81–2
    development 14, 84–5, 91, 110
    discrimination 14, 146
    minimum wage 3, 146
    monitoring 87
    motivation 88–93
    planning 154–5, 158, 159–60, 161
    recruitment 75–80
    redundancies 23
    skills 146
    stakeholders 24, 26
    turnover 14
    working conditions 3
employers: duties 3
empowerment 92
entrepreneurs
    attributes 6–7
    motivators 2–4
    skills 1, 5–6
environment 3, 12, 13, 68, 149
Equality Act 2010 14, 146
ethics 3–4, 13
executive summary 159
expenses 131
external influences 143–51
factoring 113
fashions/trends 32, 44, 148
field market research 35–7
finance 5, 25, 26, 112–39
    aims and objectives 12
    funding 18–19, 112–16, 138, 153–4
    planning 153–4, 157–8, 161
    terms and calculations 117–20
financial documents 124–34
flat organisations 21
focus groups 36

franchises 16, 17, 19
funding 18–19, 112–16, 138, 153–4
geographical expansion 106
government 16, 25, 26, 27
    reports 38
grants 115
gross domestic product (GDP) 144
growth of business 105–10, 150–1
health and safety 147
Herzberg's two-factor theory 93
hierarchies 21–2
hire purchase 138–9
human resources 75–93, 110, 154
import quotas 110
income statement 130–2
induction training 85
innovation 67
interest rates 145
interviews 37, 79
intranet 76
IT skills 5–6
job advertisements 75–8, 79
job centres 78
job description 78
joint ventures 107
just-in-time (JIT) production 98, 109
kaizen 99
lean production 98–9
leasing 114
legislation 44, 68, 110, 146–7
liabilities 123, 133
limited liability 16, 17, 19
    partnerships 18, 19
liquidity 12
    ratios 136–7
loans 26, 114, 115, 138
local businesses 13, 14
loss 120
loss leader pricing 46
loyalty
    brand 71–2
    schemes 56
management skills 5
market analysis 160
market research 34–40
market share 13, 67, 69
market types 41
market-oriented business 42
marketing mix 43–62, 65, 160
    place 43, 48–9
    price 43, 44–7, 65
    product 43, 60–2, 65
    promotion 43, 50–9, 65

Index

markets 41
    entering new 66, 67, 106, 151
Maslow's hierarchy of needs 92–3
mass markets 41
mentoring 85, 156–7
mergers 106–7
minimum wage 3, 146
mission statements 10
motivation 2–4, 88–93
needs: Maslow's hierarchy 92–3
net profit margin 135
niche markets 41
non-current (fixed) assets 123
non-current liabilities 123
objectives 9–15, 24, 25, 27
    SMART 155
observations 35–6
operations management 96–103
organisational structures 20–3
outsourcing 96–7
overdrafts 113
ownership 16–20
partnerships 16, 17, 18, 24
    limited liability 18, 19
patents 68
pay 81, 82, 88–90
    minimum wage 3, 146
penetration pricing 46
performance-related pay 89
person specification 78
place 43, 48–9
planning 153–62
population changes 44
price 32, 43, 44–7, 65
    brand image 70
    equilibrium 45
    skimming 46
pricing
    cost-plus 45
    dynamic 45
    strategies 46–7, 65
primary market research 35–7
private limited companies 16, 17, 19, 20
private sector 16
production methods 101

product(s) 43, 60–2
    -oriented business 42
    business growth 105–6
    complementary 44
    development 34, 60, 65, 67, 69, 105–6
    life cycle 63–5
    lifespan and spare parts 68
    patents 68
    portfolio 69
    range 32
profiling 56, 61, 66, 71
profit 2, 120, 124
    gross 117
    maximisers 12
    net 118
    retained 116
    sharing 90
profitability ratios 135–6
promotion 43, 50–9, 65
    mix 58
    objectives 59
promotional pricing 47
public limited companies 16, 17, 19, 20
public sector 16
qualitative data 39–40
quality 32, 62, 70, 96
    maintain and improve 99–100
quantitative data 40
questionnaires 35
ratio analysis 135–7, 157–8
recessions 144, 145, 146
recruitment 75–80
redundancies 23
references 79
remuneration 81, 82, 88–90
    minimum wage 3, 146
reorganisations 23
reputation 13, 70
resources 11, 155, 158
return on capital employed (ROCE) 136
revenue 12, 117, 124
risk(s) 34, 60, 156–7
    -taking 7–8

sales
    promotions 53–6
    revenue 117, 124
    skills 5
secondary market research 38–40
self-reflection 7
shareholders 25, 116
skills 146
    entrepreneurs 1, 5–6
small businesses 51, 77
    aims and objectives 9
    grants 115
    niche markets 41
    outsourcing 96
social and ethical motivators 3–4
social media 39, 49, 51–2, 58, 77
sole traders 16, 18, 24, 96
span of control 21–2
sponsorship 56
stakeholders 24–7, 133
start-up costs 121, 161
statement of financial position 133
stock 98, 122, 123
substitute goods 44
suppliers 26
supply 32, 45
surveys 35, 103
sustainability 3, 13–14, 149
takeovers 107
tall organisations 21, 22
taxation 143–4
    import tariffs 110
team-working 91–2
technology 110, 137, 148
temporary contract 81
text messages 57–8
timekeeping 6
trade credit 113, 138
training 14, 84–5, 91, 110
trends/fashions 32, 44, 148
unique selling point (USP) 60
unlimited liability 16, 18
working capital 133, 136–7
zero-hours contracts 82